A short account of the declaration, given by the Chinese Emperour Kam Hi, in the year 1700.

Eighteenth Century
Collections Online
Print Editions

Gale ECCO Print Editions

Relive history with *Eighteenth Century Collections Online*, now available in print for the independent historian and collector. This series includes the most significant English-language and foreign-language works printed in Great Britain during the eighteenth century, and is organized in seven different subject areas including literature and language; medicine, science, and technology; and religion and philosophy. The collection also includes thousands of important works from the Americas.

The eighteenth century has been called "The Age of Enlightenment." It was a period of rapid advance in print culture and publishing, in world exploration, and in the rapid growth of science and technology – all of which had a profound impact on the political and cultural landscape. At the end of the century the American Revolution, French Revolution and Industrial Revolution, perhaps three of the most significant events in modern history, set in motion developments that eventually dominated world political, economic, and social life.

In a groundbreaking effort, Gale initiated a revolution of its own: digitization of epic proportions to preserve these invaluable works in the largest online archive of its kind. Contributions from major world libraries constitute over 175,000 original printed works. Scanned images of the actual pages, rather than transcriptions, recreate the works *as they first appeared.*

Now for the first time, these high-quality digital scans of original works are available via print-on-demand, making them readily accessible to libraries, students, independent scholars, and readers of all ages.

For our initial release we have created seven robust collections to form one the world's most comprehensive catalogs of 18th century works.

Initial Gale ECCO Print Editions collections include:

History and Geography
Rich in titles on English life and social history, this collection spans the world as it was known to eighteenth-century historians and explorers. Titles include a wealth of travel accounts and diaries, histories of nations from throughout the world, and maps and charts of a world that was still being discovered. Students of the War of American Independence will find fascinating accounts from the British side of conflict.

Social Science

Delve into what it was like to live during the eighteenth century by reading the first-hand accounts of everyday people, including city dwellers and farmers, businessmen and bankers, artisans and merchants, artists and their patrons, politicians and their constituents. Original texts make the American, French, and Industrial revolutions vividly contemporary.

Medicine, Science and Technology

Medical theory and practice of the 1700s developed rapidly, as is evidenced by the extensive collection, which includes descriptions of diseases, their conditions, and treatments. Books on science and technology, agriculture, military technology, natural philosophy, even cookbooks, are all contained here.

Literature and Language

Western literary study flows out of eighteenth-century works by Alexander Pope, Daniel Defoe, Henry Fielding, Frances Burney, Denis Diderot, Johann Gottfried Herder, Johann Wolfgang von Goethe, and others. Experience the birth of the modern novel, or compare the development of language using dictionaries and grammar discourses.

Religion and Philosophy

The Age of Enlightenment profoundly enriched religious and philosophical understanding and continues to influence present-day thinking. Works collected here include masterpieces by David Hume, Immanuel Kant, and Jean-Jacques Rousseau, as well as religious sermons and moral debates on the issues of the day, such as the slave trade. The Age of Reason saw conflict between Protestantism and Catholicism transformed into one between faith and logic -- a debate that continues in the twenty-first century.

Law and Reference

This collection reveals the history of English common law and Empire law in a vastly changing world of British expansion. Dominating the legal field is the *Commentaries of the Law of England* by Sir William Blackstone, which first appeared in 1765. Reference works such as almanacs and catalogues continue to educate us by revealing the day-to-day workings of society.

Fine Arts

The eighteenth-century fascination with Greek and Roman antiquity followed the systematic excavation of the ruins at Pompeii and Herculaneum in southern Italy; and after 1750 a neoclassical style dominated all artistic fields. The titles here trace developments in mostly English-language works on painting, sculpture, architecture, music, theater, and other disciplines. Instructional works on musical instruments, catalogs of art objects, comic operas, and more are also included.

A

Short Account

OF THE

DECLARATION,

Given by the

CHINESE Emperour

Kam Hi,

In the Year 1700.

Nos autem predicamus Chriſtum Crucifixum.

But we do Preach Chriſt Crucify'd. 1 Cor. 23.

LONDON:

Printed in the Year MDCCIII.

THE
PREFACE.

THat the Enemies of Gods Church shou'd openly exclaim against the Society is no surprize, since these latter heresies had no sooner a birth, but God providentially rais'd it, as he had done in other times others, to oppose them with all vigour, *Offic. S. Ign.* and might therefore be well look'd lect. 5. upon as their Profess'd Adve.saries, attacking them on all sides without cease; but it is a great one, and scarce conceivable, how men of their own belief, men of Probity, Religion, and Conscience, who make it their business to distinguish themselves from the rest of Mankind by an *Air of Reformation*, and *Piety*, shoud libellously traduce them, condemn their conduct, and treat them as Idolaters, tho' to their own, not the Societies confusion.

For tho' they may prevail with their exclamations of abominations of the *Missioners* of the *Society* in China, upon the unthinking part of the World, that is prejudic'd against them for fashion sake, and thereby the easilyer dispos'd to receive any false and incoherent impressions of them, yet so long as there remains any man of good sense in the World, he will not easily believe the Fathers

will

PREFACE.

will betray the interest of that Religion, to maintain which, they sacrifice their Lives, and that they will leave all that is dear to them in Europe, and go to China with Thuribles in their hands to adore the fabulous Dieties of the East, or to frame for that vast Empire a new monstrous system of Religion, Compounded of Christianity and Heathenism, or that such able Divines, as a Richi, a Scal, a Verbiest, a Martini, fervourous zealous, Religious Missioners, whose names were no less considerable in China, than in Europe, who traverse so vast a tract of Seas to convert Infidels, should be guilty of such gross Errours, and so foreign from the purity of our Faith, and peculiar Spirit of the Society; which is to preserve our Holy Faith, in its purity among Catholicks, to defend it against its open Enemies, to oppose it self strenuously against novel opinions, and to carry it to the utmost confines of the Earth; and hence perpetual persecution becomes their lot, a signal Testimony of their still retaining their primitive Spirit.

But because there is no Calumny so coarse, which passion may not colour with the air of truth, to clear the Society, instruct the Ignorant, edify the good, and silence the Enemies of the Society, 'twas thought expedient to procure and publish this Declaration of the Emperour of China, whereby it will clearly appear, that those first Missioners were not mistaken in the strict scrutiny they made into the Chinese ceremonies and customs, And that altho his Holiness upon further examination should

sup-

PREFACE.

suppress the practice of the Society in China for the future, the Publick cannot in justice, and prudence condemn their Conduct. For what better course than theirs, could be taken by zealous and prudent Missioners at their first arrival into an Empire, regulated by Laws, Discipline, and Sciences of a quite different complexion from ours? Must they without further ceremony subvert all that is opposite to our customs, and pull up without making distinction the Tares with the good Corn? No certainly; for they go thither to conquer their Souls, not to disorder their Government.

And for their so doing, they have the Authority, Declaration, and Approbation of the Holy See of Rome, viz. that the superstitious actions may be retrenched, and those that are not superstitious, practised. The Orders of the Congregation to the Bishops in their Mission to China, *run thus:* Never perswade the people to renounce their Natural Rites, unles manifestly obnoxious to Religion, and good manners ; in effect, what is more Foreign to good sense, than to endeavour, as one wou'd say, to Frenchify *China,* to change it into *Spanish, Italian,* or to endeavour to resemble it to any Province of *Europe?* our Faith alone, and not our Manners, is to be introduc'd. For all men having an inbred inclination to value, and love their own Nation, better than others, nothing can render us more odious to this people, than

A 3 to

PREFACE.

to go about to abolish their customs, especially such as are immemorial. *And for their farther direction, whensoever it shall be doubtful, whether their Ceremonies, and Rites be purely civil and political, or superstitious, and contrary to Faith, and good Manners, the Missioner is to censure them* allowable *according to the rule prescrib'd him by the Sacred Congregation, viz.* provided they be not most openly contrary, to Religion and good Manners.

Now for some to reply, that the Chinese *ceremonies are as evidently superstitious, as it is evident,* the Seine runs by Paris, *is a bolt soon shot, for how can the Sacred Congregation believe it? since more then a hundred Missioners,* men of *Learning, Virtues, and Zeal, after all their endeavours spent for a whole Century in studying the Language, and the Genuine signification of their* Rites, Ceremonies, *and* Words, *according to their* first primitive institution, *and of consulting likewise their ablest and most intelligent* Doctors *of these* Rites, &c. for 20, or 30 Years *successively, could never perceive this clear evidence.*

Again, if it be as Evident, that Confucius *and the Dead are Idols, as it is that the* Seine runs by Paris, *how could their Adversaries connive at the Christians paying them publick respect so many years. Sixteen years are past and more, since Monsieur* Megrot *was Apostolical Vicar, who did for nine years allow the Christi-*

ans

PREFACE.

ans of his District to honour Confucius, and perform the Ceremonies of the Dead; which if manifest Idolatry, how came he to tolerate so long their so doing, without betraying his trust, and of incurring the repute of a Prevaricator, an Idolater, and a Traytor to his Religion? whereas the allowing of them can be no reproach to the Society; Because they look upon them as a civil Politick worship, and as such, allow them; so that if they be in an errour, at least they proceed Bona fide, which cannot excuse these Gentlemen, for they will never make the World believe they wanted Twelve, or Fifteen years of continual study to discover a truth, as well known to China, as 'tis to the Parisians, that the Seine runs by Paris.

The Society therefore having again fully examin'd with all candour and Sincerity the Chinese Ceremonies, and consider'd without prepossession, what was fit to allow for Publick Edification, and purity of Faith; and having prov'd in the Ballance of the Sanctuary, the most Effectual and apposite means to advance Religion in this great Empire, judged it their incumbent Duty to re-settle the Order, that had been observ'd with good Success for a whole Age, and which Rome hath permitted, and approv'd for above 40 Years. And if the best expedient to put an End to these disputes so Odious to China, and Scandalous to Europe, be, as some have thought, to permit some Ceremonies,

and

PREFACE.

And prohibit others; what more than this doth the Society at present desire, it being what they have practised for an Age.

For they forbid the Ceremonies of the E-quinox, when Wine, Meat, and Perfumes are presented after such a mode, as might Scandelize the Weak, they never allow the Burning of Paper upon Tombs, being a Bonzian Superstition, nor ever countenanc'd the pouring out of Wine upon the Coffins of the Dead; or the Elevating Eatables in the Air with Sacrificial Terms; or the trying the goodness of Beasts, by pouring Wine, or Water into their Ears; or the Hyperbolizing in the encomiums of Confucius; as being not Ignorant, that most of these additional Ceremonies, tho indifferent in themselves, are shocking, especially to us Europeans, unacquainted with the True Reason, and meaning of them. And of all the Honours by Law Establish'd, in Favour of Confucius, they only Tollerate such as are us'd by Bachellours of Art; and which consist solely in prostrating before his Name, in token of the respect that is due to him, still retaining it, as a principle amongst them Confucius is but a Man: The Learned make him their Master, not their God. If likewise you inquire of the Chinese about their Ceremonies perform'd to the Dead: They, as well as their several Ancient and approv'd Antiquaries, will assure you, that nothing remains of a Dead man in the Grave, but his Body, And that the Soul mounts up to

Hea-

PREFACE.

Heaven, and refides there. *And that thefe Ceremonies are merely intended, Firft, As tokens of gratitude, and payments of that Duty and Reverence, which is due from Children to Parents, and are, Secondly, Their Monuments, erected for no other End, then to perpetuate in their Families, the Memory of their Progenitors, efpecially the Raifers, and the more Eminent of their progeny.*

In order therefore to their vindication from the unjuft Cenfure they have been branded with, and may perhaps again, they have this to offer to the unprejudiced Reader ; that if, as men, they have err'd, they have prudently err'd, as having followed in the queft of truth fuch rules as Chriftian Prudence, and Right Reafon Dictates in all mens opinion ; for it is certain, the Jefuites for thefe hundred years have confulted the ableft men in the Empire, as Minifters of State, Governours of Provinces, Vice-Roys, learned and celebrated Doctors, and moft of them Chriftians, and confequently the moft competent judges to know and diftinguifh Civil from Religious worfhip. The more therefore they confidered the matter, the more they were convinc'd of the neceffity of ftanding by their firft Decifions. And tho' fome Miffioners of other Bodies were of a different Judgment, yet the moft learned of the Dominicans fubfcribed to the Fathers, even againft their own Brethren. And two of their Provincials after a rigorous difcuffion of the queftion, ordered their Subjects to fide with them

PREFACE.

them. But what is, and ought to be the most convincing Argument to determine the matter is this late Declaration of the Emperour of China, &c. the chief Subject matter of this Book. And what above all they have to offer in their vindication, and that assures them, they are in the right, is the Declaration of Rome it self in their favour, after having heard both Parties.

And what else do they now desire, but the continuance of the same method thus so many ways, and so Solidly authoriz'd? And what other methods have, I pray, their present Adversaries observ'd since their Mission? Was it not in Virtue of the second Decree of the Sacred Congregation, they were oblig'd to admit the Politicbites, and reject the Superstitions? Have not both Parties liv'd quietly so long together, and animated with the same spirit, labour'd for the same end? Have not these new Apostles been edify'd with their zeal, incourag'd by their example, and supported by their Authority, lead their flocks with them to the same pasture, and march'd the same way, which the supreme Pastor Alexander VII had chalk'd out to all? and this under the favour, and protection of the Emperour, whom we hope to see in time become the great Constantine of Asia, if these new revev'd disputes, carried on with over-acted zeal, and inconsiderate heats, do not (which God avert) unhappily obstruct it. But for the excesses of others, the Society is not to be answerable; For must they to allay the Storm, and

to

PREFACE.

to gratify the unwarrantable humour of a few modern Missioners, ruin and lay wast, what fifty others more ancient, and better vers'd in the Mission, have so wisely establish'd? Must they run the risque not only of their own reputation, but what is far more, of Religion, and the conversion of the greatest Empire of the Universe: This would prove to be a more fatal peace, than War. And after all, it is much to be doubted; whether it could be maintain'd long upon such terms, without the raising of new Controversies.

Tho' this must be said in their Commendation, that to all the crimes laid to their charge, they have never recriminated. They could have put a bar to the new Mission in China, and covertly have defeated the accusation with the Accuser: but far from such proceedings, tho not impracticable, they have been more than once imploy'd in their behalf, and their own hand will attest, how the Society hath shelter'd them under its wings, as F. Alcala a Dominican testifies in his letter at Manila on this Subject; where he extolls the indefatigable labours of the Society in China, and ingeniously owns, that the other Missioners without their protection would have been incapacitated to discharge their function. They have seconded their good intentions, concur'd to their Settlement, and have not only sacrifis'd their resentments for the love of Jesus Christ, but also their own private interests, tho they well foresaw, it wou'd turn in the end to their disadvantage.

The

PREFACE.

The ſole thought, that Divine Providence will
in due time direct all to a bleſſing, and edifying
peace, anticipates their joy in the midſt of
their ſufferings. This peace ſo precious in the
ſight of God, ſo neceſſary for each Parties repoſe,
and ſo advantagous for the converſion of Idolaters, have they coveted, tho loden with Ca-
lumnies, and have waited for with patience, and
good Offices. And whoſoever at unawars any
word of complaint dropt from their Lips, 'twas
not ſo much the reſentment of their ſufferings, as
the regret for the troubles, and deſolation of the
Church.

    For they are very ſenſible, the greateſt E-
vil derives its Origin from the common
Enemy of Peace and Religion. The Divil ever
bent upon michief, in order to worry the Flock
of Chriſt, leaves no ſtone unturn'd to divide the
Paſtorrs. To raiſe commotions amongſt World-
lings, he ſets all their Humours aflote; and
to diſturb the Zealous Miſſioners in the Mi-
niſtry, he miſuſes their Virtue, Scandal is Var-
niſh'd with the Colour of Zeal, and the Spirit of
Reformation ſtops the Current of the Goſpol. The
Ambition of ſharing in the Apoſtolical Labours of the Society has ſuberted the Occonomy
of their Miſſions, and thus Hell Encounters
them with their Arms. Theſe conſiderations
make the Society willing to defend its Adver-
ſaries, and ſhould be tranſported with Joy to
ſee them linck'd to it with the Bonds of Charity. It readily apologizes for the weakneſs of

ſome

PREFACE.

some few, applauding their good intentions. The thing alone it desires is, that all prejudice may be laid aside, and a right Idea of Idolatry, so much of late in mens Mouths, re-assum'd then they'll be easiely convinc'd, that it is only a fancy of their own Brains, which a little charity would correct, did but every one let fall the interest of his Party.

For who can without regret hear them say in Asia, and even in Europe, and nearer home, I am Paul's, I am Apollo's, and I am Cephas's, what imports it, whether our Faith be preached by Cephas, or Apollo? All is good, all is profitable, provided our Lords name be announc'd to the whole World; All are Christs Ministers, but then let them not divide Jesus Christ by dangerous debates, nor turn the sword given them for the destruction of Infernal powers against his Ministers. It is very true, that even the first Apostles were not all of a mind; that St. Paul reprimanded St. Peter, and that the same Apostle not long after left St. Barnaby upon light grounds in appearance; And in a Controversy between St. Jerom, and St. Austin; there was a certain air of animosity, to convince us, the greatest Saints have not quite shaken off the old man. In a word, much Zeal, and little discretion may cause great Scandal in the Church, and makes the reproach fall heavy on those that were the first authors of such hot and stubborn debates; who with the Scandal thence arising, wound the very Souls, they meant to cure.

How

PREFACE.

How aptly are a_iplyed to such these words of St. *Paul*, nonne delictum est in 1 Cor. 6. vobis, quod judicia habetis inter vos? Quare non injuriam magis accipitis? Sed vos injuriam facitis, & hoc fratribus. *Pretend what you will, is it not a fault to Entertain, and foment differences amongst you? why do you not rather put up the Affront? Far from bearing it patiently, you attack each other, even your own Brethren. How far better were it, and more edifying to own and say,* Frater es, crescas in Mille millia. *These are my Brethren, may they increase more and more, to the greater Glory of God, and the good of his Holy Church. Their Honour shall be to me as deer as my own, these are Ministers of Jesus Christ, replenish'd with zeal, Capacity, and Probity, who have born for a whole Age, the Weight, and Heat of the Day in our Lords Vineyard, to whose experience in this Mission I ought, as less acquainted with the Customs, Ceremonies, and Genious of this Nation, to supersede. Thus all animated with each others Zeal, will Labour unanimously to fill up* Christ's *Fold, and these are the true desires the love of Religion inspires his Missioners, with for the conversion of* China.

And here I purpos'd to have put an End to this Preface, *but upon Second thoughts, I have drawn it out much beyond my First intention, with the Transactions and Decisions*

of

PREFACE.

of Rome, *upon the Questions in debate; which will, I hope, both please the Readers, who have hitherto talkt* Pro *and* Con *of the matter without Book, and together plead the Pardon of a prolix* Preface

After then that the Fathers had for 50 Years Laboured with great Success in this new Planted Vineyard of Christ, to the Astonishment of all. F. John Baptist de Morales a Dominican Fryar *and* F. Anthony de sante Maria, *a* Franciscan, *having been about 3 or 4 Years in* China, *and perfectly learnt, as they fancyed the* Chinese *Language, began to Scrupulize the practise of the Fathers of the Society, and to disturb the Peace of this Florishing Mission. For without any regard or difference had to the plurality of Missioners, grown already grey in the Study of the* Chinese Characters, *they began to boggle at their Method; and writ immediately to the* Philippin-Islands, *that* they had seen Abomination of Desolation in the Holy place; *that Christianity was prophaned, and that the Ministers of Jesus Christ, instead of beating down Idolatry, defended it. This letter made a great noise in those Islands, and two of the Bishops,* viz. *the* Arch-Bishop *of* Manila, *and the Bishop of* Zebut, *more zelous than the rest, thought fit to give the,* Pope Urban *the* VIII. *on account of what was writ to them from* China, *and hotly accus'd the Missioners of the Society, of introducing practises contrary to Ecclesiastical* Customs, *and the purity*

of

PREFACE.

of our Faith. *But these BB. upon better infor-*
mations, they receiv'd in a second letter, repen-
ted, and own'd they had been misinform'd. And
as it was the duty of a Bishop to attack errours
dressed out in any disguise, so it was a point of
Justice in them to patronise innocency, and dis-
countenance calumny. We are, say they, o-
blig'd in *Conscience* to justify the *Fathers* of
the *Society* against such unjust accusations,
and exert our utmost endeavours to defend
the Truth, and their Innocency. *And with*
this Authentick Declaration, the Tempest seem'd
to be Allay'd. But Father Morales, *to con-*
vince the World of the Fathers ill proceedings,
being now Embarkt in the debate, thought him-
self oblig'd to push it on. Wherefore without
staying in China *for the clearing of his doubts*
there, tho' he had propos'd them to the Visi-
tour of the Society, he unknown to them, as
to his Voyage and design, Imbarks for Europe,
comes to Rome, *about the End of the Ponti-*
ficate of Urban VIII. *and proposes his doubts*
in 17 *Articles to the Congregation of Cardinals;*
which are, as follows.

1. *Whether the* Chinese Christians *be bound*
to fast, keep the Precepts of the Church, confess,
and communicate once a year?

2. *Whether the Missioners in the Baptism*
of Women, may omit the Ceremonies of Spittle,
Salt, and the Oyl of Catechumens, or dispense
with the administration of Extrema-Unction *to*
them?

2. *Whe-*

PREFACE.

3. Whether it may be allowed the Chinese, to take 30 p. Cent, according to the Imperial Statute forloan of money, lying dead by them and without hazard of the principle?

4. Whether it be lawful to permit publick Uferers, turning Christians, to continue their Ufury, when fo oblig'd by the Manderins.

5. Whether Children be bound to roftore the ufarous gain?

6. Whether, when the Idolators collect contribution in Cities and Towns for heathenifh Sacrifices, and fuperftitions, the Chriftians may contribute their quota for fear of incuring the Pagans Hatred and Difpleafure, in cafe of refufal?

7. Whether, becaufe the Manderins are oblig'd on certain exigencies to Sacrifice to the Idol Chim-hoan, to proftrate before it, to adore it, the Chriftians in office may be allow'd at their entering their Temples, to conceal a crofs in their hand, or in the flowers of the Altar, and fo perform all their exteriour Rites, under pretence of referring mentally, the honour not to the Idol, but to the crofs hidden.

8. Whether Chriftians can offer Sacrifice to Confucius in his Temple, affift at it, or make ufe of a Crofs to direct their intention by?

9. Whether the like oblations being offered to the Dead, the Chriftians may be prefent, and make thefe offerings, intending them as before, to the conceal'd Crofs?

10 Whether one may not tollerate the Chri-

a   ftians

PREFACE.

ſians to perform in private the above menti-
oned Ceremonies, without any other then meer
civil reſpect to their Progenitors, eſpecially if a
Croſs accompany the offering?

11 Whether, it being a Chineſe cuſtom in
this occaſion to have a penſil tablet, call'd in
their Tongue the ſeat of the Soul, the place,
where the Soul does really repoſe, and accept the oblations, proſtretion, and Prayers of
her Votaries, and is plac'd on a real Altar,
can a Chriſtian retain theſe reſemblances, and
uſe them with their Ceremonies?

12 Whether when one dies, an Altar is
erected in the Houſe near the Coffin, Perfume,
and wax Lights burn in his Honour, there hangs
a Tablet, where the Parents and Relations pro-
ſtrate to, &c. all this be lawful?

13 Whether it be neceſſary to inſtruct the
Catechumens before Baptiſm, that Chriſtian
Religion prohibits all Sacrifices, and Idola-
try?

14 Whether XIM, ſignifying with the
Chineſe the ſame, as Saint with us, one may
uſe it to humour the Idolaters, and ſay, Confucius is a Saint?

15 Whether it be allowable to our Miſſioners
to place in our Churches on the Altars Chineſe-
riſe, a picture with this inſcription, let the
Emperour live a Thouſand and a Thouſand
Years?

16 Whether one may ſay Maſs for the
Chineſe Idolaters, that dyed in their Infidelity?

17. Whe

PREFACE.

17 *Whether they being scandaliz'd at our preaching Jesus Christ crucified, it be necess. to mention this Mystery, or shew them a Crucifix?*

These, Reader, are the doubts, which F Jo. Baptist de Morales had observ'd and collected after three or four years of superficial study of the Chiness *knotty Sciences, Mysties, and Rites. And not being able himself to decide such obvious Catechistical instructions, he judg'd it his duty to take a second tour about the World to consult the Sacred Congregation, whether Christians show'd be prohibited usurerious practices, or might offer Sacrifice to Idols? or whether it were lawful to dissemble ones Religion, appearing an Idolater in publick, provided one ador'd the true God in private? whether one might pray for the Damned, or Canonize notorious Infidels after death? or whether a Christian might be lawfully ignorant of Jesus Christ Crucified?*

But this good Father might have added one quere more for the quiet of his Conscience, and ask'd the Congregation, whether it were lawful for a Religious man, a Priest, and a Missioner to arraign before the highest Court of Judicature in Gods *Church his Brethren of prevarication, superstition, and Idolatry, without good grounds? It had been more to his purpose to have been resolv'd of this doubt, and being inform'd of his obligation in this case, he might have sav'd himself the pains of proposing his*

queres

PREFACE.

enquires to the sacred Congregation. For it is clear that this good man meant to accuse the Missioners of the Society, tho no mention be made of them in the process; and would have the World believe them guilty, or at least thought so, of these abominations, as appears by his own letter, and private conferences.

The Missioners in China having receiv'd intelligence of these transactions in Europe, deputed F. Martini of their Society, to inform the Court of Rome of the true State of the Missions; who at his arrival explain'd the particular customs of China to the Pope and Cardinals, their Laws, Policy, and Religion, together with what the Missioners of the Society tolerated in the Chinese Neophites. And in the winding up of his discourse, beg'd the favour of his Holyness to prescribe to their Missioners the methods they were to observe for the future. And that as he had heard F. Morales, he would vouchsafe to lend an Ear to the humble remonstrance of F. Martini which to do justice to both parties was accordingly granted, and a second Decree obtain'd.

The

PREFACE.

The Answer of the Second Congrega-
tion. An. Dom. 1656.

THE Miſſioners of the Society of Je-
ſus having not been Heard, when
ſeveral queries were propos'd to the Sacred Congregation *de propaganda,* and the
matters of Fact differently ſtated. Our
Holy Father has remitted this Affair to
the Sacred Congregation of the Supream
and General Inquiſition of Faith, which
after having reported, the ſentiments of
the Qualificatours return'd the following
Anſwers.

The Firſt demand made by F. Martini,
was to know, whether the Miſſioner, when
he Baptizes a Catechumen, be bound to
declare to him his obligation under Mortal Sin of obſerving the Poſitive Law, or
precepts of the Church, as to Faſts, Ec-
cleſiaſtical Feaſts, Annual Confeſſion, and
Eaſter Communion?

The ground of the doubt as to Faſting
is this. The *Chineſe* are accuſtom'd from
their Cradle to Three Meals a day, becauſe
their Aliments are very Light. Beſides
the *Mandarins* are oblidg'd to be at Court,
and remain there for Eight Hours together in the Morning til two in the,

After

PREFACE.

Afternoon, which to do Fasting is abfo
lutely impracticable. As to Feafts, moft
Chriftians are bound to work for their
Livelyhood. Moreover many of them are
order'd by their Mandarins to do many
Servile works upon Holy-days. And the
Mandarins themfelves are bound to a per-
fonal appearance at Court on the fame
days, upon pain of being turn'd out. The
Miffioners being few, the Kingdom vaftly
large, it is impoffible for all Chriftians to
hear Mafs on Holy-day, Confefs once a
Year, and receive at Eafter.

The Sacred Congregation, purfuant to
the Report, advifed the Miffioners to inform the Chriftians, that the pofitive
Law of the Church relating to Fafts,
obfervance of Feafts, Annual Confeffions and
Communions, oblig'd them under mortal fin,
yet at the fame time they might remonftrate
to them the Reafons, why they are Sometimes difpens'd with in the Obfervance of
thefe precepts. And that if his Holinefs
thought fit, the Miffioners might have power to difpenfe with them in particular
cafes, which they judged Neceffary.

The Second Demand Whethere the Mif-
fioner in Baptizing Women ought to ob-
ferve the Church Ceremonies? Item.
Whether it is not fit to give the Sa-
crament of Extream-Unction only to thofe
that afk it? Or even refufe it to them,
when any probabil'ty, Prophanation, or Scandal may follow, or &c. The

PREFACE.

The grounds of this demand proceed from the Extream Modesty of the *Chinese* Women, their inbred Bashfullness and great Aversion to the Commerce of men, shuning their very Sight. So that unless the Missioners carry themselves in this occasion with great reserve and precaution, they give great Scandal to the *Chinese*, and expose Religion to Eminent danger of being lost.

The Sacred Congregation, in regard to these queries, judged it expedient for us, to omit some Ceremonies in the Administration of Baptism, and to dispense with Extream Unction in case of necessity.

The Third demand Whether Christian Scholars may practise with a safe Conscience, the Ceremonies that are perform'd in Honour of *Confucius* in his Hall, at the taking their degrees, because no Sacrifice is then offer'd, no Pagan Priest, or Bonzy present, nor any Idolatrous Rites perform'd, but an Assembly only of the Learned, as Scholars, that own *Confucius* for their Master, meet and give him a civil and polite respect, in compliance with the first institution. In this Hall or Colledge, which is opened to no other People but Scholars, and by consequence no Temple, Students that are to take the degree of Batchelour meet, and attend the Chancellour, Doctors, and Examiners, and having paid their De-

c 4

vours

PREFACE.

voirs and Reverences before *Confucius's* name,
no otherwise than Scholars do to their
living Masters, and own'd him for their
Master, they are graduated by the Chancellour, and then withdraw.

The Sacred Congregation has thought
fit according to these Informations to permit the *Chinese* Christians the practice of
these ceremonies, because it seems to be a
respect and worship purely civil and politick

The fourth demand Whether it may be
permitted to the Christians to practice the
ceremonies instituted according to the
Maxims of the *Chinese* Philosophers in Honour of their Dead, rejecting the superstitions, that have been since added *Item*, whether the *Chinese* Christians may practice
these sort of permited ceremonies in company of their Pagan Parents. And more,
whether it may be allowed the *Chinese*
Christians, after having made a profession
of their Faith, to be present at the superstitious ceremonies of the Idolaters, not to
join with them in those Actions, nor Au-
thorise them, but because it would look
very strange to have Relations absent, and
dispens'd with in their civil Duties, and thus
become the occasion of Disgust, Enmity
and Hatred, in fine the *Chinese* attributes no
Divinity to the Souls of the Dead, nor
hope for, or demand any thing from them.
The

PREFACE.

The three manners they have of honouring their Dead are explain'd at length in the decree.

The Sacred Congregation pursuant to what has been propos'd has judg'd, that it might be suffered the *Chinese* Converts to practice these sorts of ceremonies in Honour of their Dead, and in company with the Gentils, provided the superstitious be cut off. *Item*, that they may assist with them at their ceremonies, that are mixt with superstitions, when they have first made their profession of Faith, and when there is no danger of their perversion, and when they cannot otherwise avoid the Enmity and Hatred of their Relations.

This decree was brought to the general Assembly of the Inquisition, and approved by our H Father Pope Alexander VII. Mar. 23. 1656.

F. Martini *having obtain'd it after a long debate, and a most rigid examination, return'd to* China *fully perswaded; that now the Missioners of the Gospel, cemented with the Charity of* Jesus Christ, *would for the future labour with the same Spirit, and uniformity of mind in the Conversion of this great Empire. But God, whose Judgments are unsearchable, did not permit the Adversaries of the Society to open their Eyes to the Light. It was natural enough to adhere to this last decision, opposite to the former, yet they made it a point of Conscience,*

and

PREFACE.

and perhaps of honour too, to protest against this second decree.

For when F. Morales obtain'd the first decree, the Society was not heard, as knowing nothing of his Journey to Rome, nor design; and tho it ordered the Chinese Christians to abstain from certain practices express'd in his demands, yet it was with this additional clause, *till his Holyness, or the Holy See ordains otherwise,* the reason of adding this limitation was, because they could not be assur'd, that these practices as laid down by F. Morales, were conform to the truth, and that, what was permitted in China, was so freely, as he had conceiv'd, and therefore the Sacred Congregation proceeded very wisely in making a decree, that shou'd stop the course of evil, if there was any in it, and shou'd be nevertheless *Provisional,* till the Holy See, after a more ample information, ordaineth otherwise, if necessary.

And that the practices of the Chinese Christians were not so bad, as F. Morales, hurryed on by too much zeal, and for want of longer experience, had so it conceiv'd, is clear by his own proceedings at his return to China. For of the 17 answers which he had receiv'd from the Holy See to his same number, 9 do his he thought fit to suppress, 9, viz the 4, 5, 6, 10, 12, 13, 14, 15, 16, in which he had spoken of the Baptism of publick Offices, of the restitution their Heirs ought to be oblig'd to, in lieu of the Contribution exacted of Christ ans for the Feasts

and

PREFACE.

and Sacrifices of Idols of the honour Christians pay to their Doctor Confucius, &c And of the other eight Answers, which he thought fit to publish in the Chinese language, for the instruction of Christians, he has only given a slight abstract, a clear sign of self-Conviction that he had been formerly misinformed, and that he had trusted too much to others, that knew no better the customs, and ceremonies of China, than he did himself. Does it not therefore look to have more of honour then conscience in it to stand out still, and not conform to this second decree, which was issued out after both parties had been heard, and the matters of fact candidly stated, and different from F. Morale's, and which he himself would not stand to at his return into China.

With two Notandums more I close this Preface, the first, that it is not pretended the first decree was ever absolutely repeal'd by the second, tho it was delivered with such wise caution, that it was to be in force till such time the Holy See should think fit to ordain otherwise; as defacto it did upon hearing and deciding the demands of the Society, who had not then been heard, when the first decree was procur'd Neither is it pretended that the second decree is to be exclusive of a third, if for example, truth shoud appear hereafter in a clearer light, then it does at present. But as the third won'd certainly suppose the Informations of the Society to be of little weight, so the second suppose, the

same

PREFACE.

same of the first, and abundantly satisfies the World, that the Sacred Congregation did not altogether credit the Testimony of Father John Baptist de Morales.

The second thing to be noted is, that if, under the pretext of the matter of Facts being misrepresented to the Court of Rome, one may lawfully refuse to subscribe to its decrees, as here in effect they did to this second decree, Rome can never oblige the Faithfull, tho Subjects, to stand to its decisions, for there will never be wanting this precedent for all to protest against its proceedings, viz. his Holyness was misinform'd of the fact, and thus the least tergiversation may screen them from their obedience to their Chief Pastor. It is very true, one may suspend the execution of an order upon certain emergences, especially when acquired manifestly by a false information. But what Court of Judicature can countenance disobedience to a decree of above forty years standing, no ways repugnant to truth at least in appearance? And conform to which these very Adversaries of the Society did, as I observ'd before, govern themselves and their Flock for many years. That is, till F. Joseph Monteyro, a Portugues Jesuite by order of the Arch-Bishop of Goa, intimated in his name to Monsieur Maigrot, that the present affair of the Indies being ended in favour of the Bishop of Rome by Urban VIII that Prelate had joyned him to act as his Grand Vicar in the Province of Monsieur Maigrot.

A

A

Short Account

OF THE

DECLARATION,

Given by the

CHINESE Emperour

Kam Hi,

In the Year 1700.

An Account of what happen'd before the obtaining the Emperour's Declaration.

A Dispute of Moment being rais'd about the Year 1638, concerning some customs, Establisht in the *Chinese* Empire : Some looking upon those Practices, as Superstitious, and favouring of Idolatry, which the *F. F.* of the Society had allow'd of, as Civil and Political Ceremonies. Both Parties had Recourse

B   to

to the Holy See, but at different times, in order to Learn what was to be Taught and Practis'd in a business of so great a concern. And as the Question was variously stated; so different Answers were given in Relation to the Lawfulness, and Unlawfulness of those Ceremonies, without entring upon an examine of the different matters of Fact each Party Alledg'd. A Decision of that nature requiring more time, and pains, than the matter in debate could well admit of In this Dispute the Opinion of the Society was backt by many Eminent men, weighty Reasons, and Texts of Claacle Authors, concerning which, many Treatiscs have been Publ t. But this Question being propos'd a new to the Court of *Rome*, and in all appearance not like to be ended in many Years, without much pains and labour, each endeavouring to make out by the Authority of *Chinese* Authors, that they are in the right, as to the sense and meaning of these Rites: It was thought expedient to search out some compendious way of ending this Controversy, which as on the one hand would certainly be grateful to his Holiness, who desires nothing more than their Union, and agreement, who labour in that Mission; so on the other, might be sufficient to put an end to this Dispute, which has lasted m ry Years, and quiet their Consciences, who have been in some pain about it.

In order to effect this, all the F. F residing at *Pekin*, agreed that the Emperour himself was to be consulted, and intreated to determine by a certain and safe Sentence, the true sense and
meaning

meaning of the Rites and Ceremonies of the Empire; that thence they might come to understand, whether the Ceremonies, by which *Confucius* was usually hononour'd, were only Civil duties, or in some measure Religious. Their intent, I say, was to obtain a certain and safe decision of this doubt. For it belongs to the Emperour alone to determine the Rites which are to be us'd, and the end to which they are to be directed.

For he being the Supreme Legiflator of the Empire, as well in Relation to Religious, as Civil Duties, his Authority is fo abfolute in both thefe points, that he Prefcribes to the whole Empire, the Ceremonies which are to be us'd, the end, to which they are to be directed, and the fenfe, in which the Writings of the Ancients are to be taken. His Decifion of the prefent doubt, was alfo certain to recieve no fmall Authority from the great Repute he is in through the whole Empire, for a Man profoundly Learned, and he muft effectually pafs for fuch in all men's Opinions, who confider the number of *European* and *Chinefe* Sciences, in which this Prince excells. He is fo eminent in the latter, that he examines all the Learn'd men, who refort to *Pekin*, in order to be promoted to the Supreme degree, Eftablifht in the Empire, and paffes his Judgment of the excellence of their Compofitions: In fo much, that fcarce any of his Subjects reach the Reputation he is in, as to the point of Learning and Erudition.

Now

Now in order to obtain this Princes Sentence, no small difficulties were to be surmounted. They seem'd at the first sight so very great, that some of the F. F. who at first resolv'd to have recourse to him, look'd upon them as insurmountable, and were against attempting it. The chief, which occur'd, was the dread they were in, least the Emperour, being of a sharp and piercing Wit, should endeavour to penetrate, and would absolutely know upon what account, and what intent the F. r. so unanimously Petition'd his determination concerning the point in Question, and that it seem'd very probable, that he would endeavour to find it out by many Questions, and that by that means he might come to have some knowledge of the difficulties rais'd against the Society by an Apostolical Vicar. Now if this should happen, and draw him into some inconveniencies the Society would be certainly expos'd to a great Odium, and he under the Imputation of having abus'd its power with a Heathen Prince against the Apostolical Vicars. This consideration suspended for a long time the execution of what was design'd, all concluding, that it was rather to be laid aside, then attempted with so much danger. But at length this difficulty was surmounted, and the danger remov'd, when means were found out to Petition his Majesty in such terms, as were neither liable to create any suspicion in him, or danger to others, as will appear by the Tenor of the Petition presented to him.

Upon

Upon this, the bufinefs being communicated to all the *F F* and diligently difcus'd, and that way which was propos'd, as moft fafe, examin'd with all maturity and attention, all unanimoufly concluded to Petition his Majefty in the Name of all refiding at *Pekin*, to declare to them the true fenfe and meaning of the *Chinefe* Ceremonies.

This being agreed on, after fome days fpent in imploring the Divine affiftance, and drawing up the defign'd Petition, on the 19th of *November* 1700, they intimated their defign to the *Tartar Mandarin Hesken*, by whom their Petition was to be prefented to the Emperour, and refolv'd to have it prefented on the Feaft of the Prefentation of the Bleffed Virgin. This *Mandarin* who is well verft in the affairs of *China*, and upon account of his Erudition, quick Wit, and eloquent Stile, much valued by the Emperour. was no fooner acquainted with what we defign'd to propofe to him ; but he told us without Hefitation, that the Ceremonies perform'd towards *Confucius*, and the Dead, were only Civil duties. that by their Primitive Inftitution they were directed to no other end, and that this was the fenfe of the Empire in Relation to them Being further ask'd his fentiment concerning the *Tien*, or *Heaven*, and *Xam Ti*, he prefently Anfwer'd, That he underftood the Supreme Maker, and Lord of Heaven and Earth, that the Ancient Philofophers and Kings meant the fame by them, that all things were govern'd by him, and not by the Material Heavens, or any Inanimate Being

B 3   But

But this Courtier, being like the rest in these parts, very cautious, was deterr'd from presenting our Petition to his Prince, not knowing how it would be receiv'd; for the Question seem'd too bold, and he was not dispos'd to run the least risk upon our account. Whilst he was wavering and doubtful of the reception our Petition might meet with, since it laid the Emperour, otherwise Impenetrable, under a necessity of declaring publickly, whether he Ador'd the true God of Heaven and Earth, or only the Material Heaven. The Eunuch *Le* (one of those few, who always attend the Emperour, and carries his Orders) gave him a visit, *Howard* he being intimate Friends, he propos'd the business to him, in order to have his Advice: He reciev'd the happiest Answer he could wish for, being told that he might safely, and without danger propose what we desir'd, to the Emperour. These few words did not only free the *Tartar Mandarine* from his doubts, but made him active in the business, being very willing to embrace any occasion of pleasing his Master. Now whilst we were labouring with him to do our Petition into the *Tartar* Language, the Emperour went with his Court to visit the River *Tum Tm Ho.* But this accident, which seem'd Inconvenient, turn'd rather to the best For the *Tart. Mandarin* being left at home, and being at leisure during the Prince's absence; he did our Petition out of the *Chinese* Paper, containing only the chief heads of what was to be propos'd, into the *Tartar* Tongue

The

The Emperour return'd on the 28th of *November*, and no opportunity prefenting it felf the following day, on the 30th of the fame Month, being St. *Andrew*'s Day, Five Fathers of the Society met at the Palace, *viz. F. Philippe Grimaldi*, Rector of the College, *F. Thomas Pereyra, F. Antony Thomas, F. John Gerbillon*, and *F. Joachim Bouvet*, and in the name of all the Fathers refiding at *Pekin*, prefented their Petition to the Emperour by two Court *Mandarins*, Namely, *Hisko*, and his Companion *Cham Cham Chu*, it was the 20th day of the 10th Moon, and the 39th Year of the Reign of the Emperour *Kam Hi*. In his prefence they fpoke as follows in our Name.

'That we had reciev'd Letters out of *Europe*, 'by which we underftood, that they were well 'acquainted there, with what Fame had fpread 'far and near, concerning the admirable Magna- 'nimity, Wifdom, perfect Underftanding of 'Books, and admirable Learning, in which his '*Chinese* Majefty excell'd. But the Learned there 'not underftanding the meaning of the *Chinese* 'Rites and Sacrifices, they defir'd us to fend 'them an Explanation of them. But becaufe 'thefe Rites belong to the Cuftoms of the Em- 'pire, and we doubt whether or no we have ex- 'actly expreft its fenfe in relation to them; we 'durft not rely upon the Anfwer we defign'd to 'give them, unlefs approv'd of by his Majefty, 'whom we therefore intreated to inftruct us con- 'cerning them.

B 4   The

The Emperour having heard this Account of the bufinefs, took and perus'd attentively our Petition in the chief Hall of his Palace, call'd *Kien Cim Cim*, about Eight in the Morning. The Contents were as follows.

---

§. II.

The Petition offer'd to the Emperour Kam Hi, *on the 30th of* November, 1700 *in which certain Rites and Cuftoms of the* Chinefe, *are Explain'd in the fame fenfe, in which the Society hath hitherto allow'd the practice of them*

Altho' the Learn'd Men of *Europe* have heard of the Rites, by which the *Chinefe* honour *Heaven, Confucius,* and their deceas'd Parents; yet not knowing to what thefe Rites tend, they have Written to us in the following terms.

‘ Whereas the Benignity and Munificence of
‘ the Great Emperour of *China* has reach'd all
‘ Countries, and the Fame of his admirable Wif-
‘ dom hath been fpread thro' all Kingdoms, it
‘ feems certain to us, that the Rites and Cuftoms
‘ in ufe amongft his People, muft be grounded on
‘ fome weighty reafons, wherefore we defire
‘ you would fend an exact and diftinct account of
‘ them. We anfwer as follows.

‘ When

'When the *Chinese* honour *Confucius*, their
'defign is to exprefs their Reverence towards
'him for the Doctrine deliver'd to them, which
'fince they reciev'd from him, how can they do
'otherwife than return him due Honour for it,
'by bended Knees, and Heads bow'd down to
'the Ground? This is the true fence and reafon
'which moves the *Chinefe* Empire to Efteem and
'Reverence *Confucius*, in Quality of its Mafter;
'and the genuine fenfe and meaning of the refpect
'this Nation pays him, by which they never de-
'fign to beg of him Wit, a clear Underftanding,
'or Preferment. The Ceremonies perform'd by
'them towards their deceas'd Parents and Rela-
'tions, are only us'd by them as Teftimonies, of
'the Love and Reverence they owe them, and as
'greatful acknowledgments towards the Heads of
'their Families. For this intent, the Ancient
'Emperours prefcrib'd certain Solemn Rites, by
'which the Dead are to be Honour'd at certain
'Seafons, *viz.* in Summer and Winter; as well
'Parents by their Children, as other near Rela-
'tions and Friends, by thofe, who upon account
'of Kindred, or Friendfhip, were particularly
'United to them. Now the Sole end and defign
'of this Inftitution, was to Eftablifh a method of
'expreffing their great Love and Affection to-
'wards them, as far as it could poffibly be ex-
'preft.
'We fay that the Sacrifices which the Ancient
'Kings and Emperours us'd to offer to Heaven,
'are the fame with thofe which the *Chinefe* Philo-
'fophers call *Kiao Xe*, that is, Sacrifices offer'd
'to Heaven and Earth, by which they fay, that
'*Xam Ti*, or the Supreme Lord of Heaven and
'Earth

'Earth is Worſhipped. Upon this account the
'Inſcription, before which theſe Sacrifices are
'offer'd, contains theſe words, *Xam Ti*, that is
'to the Supreme Lord Hence it is evident that
'theſe Sacrifices are not directed to the viſible
'and material Heaven, but to the ſupreme Lord
'and Maſter of Heaven and Earth, and all things
'elſe, whom when thro' reſpect they forbear to
'call by his proper name, they ſtile the Supreme
'Heaven, the Beneficial Heaven, the Univerſal
'Heaven, *&c.* which figurative expreſſion they
'frequently uſe in relation to the Emperour him-
'ſelf, when out of reverence to him they omit that
'Title, and uſe theſe expreſſions, *beneath the*
'*ſteps of his Throne, the cover Hill of his Pa-*
'*lace,* &c which expreſſions, tho' different as to
'words, ſignify the ſelf ſame thing

'Hence is alſo evident, that the Writing his
'Majeſty honour'd us with, in which he Wrote
'with his own hand, *Kem Tien*, worſhip Heaven
'bears no other ſenſe than the mention'd. We
'Externs, and your Majeſty's Subjects not being
'well vers'd in theſe Rites, and not knowing
'how far this expoſition of the *Chineſe* cuſtom is
'conſonant to Truth, humbly beg your Majeſty
'will pleaſe to impart to us your Royal Inſtruc-
'tions, and correct this our Anſwer, in caſe it be
'found to differ from the true ſenſe and meaning
'of the *Chineſe* Nation This expoſition of the
Chineſe Rites having been Read, and attentively
conſider'd, the Emperour gave the following Anſwer in the *Tarta* Tongue.

'The

' The Contents of this Writing are well Writ-
' ten, and agree perfectly with the great Doctrine.
' All Nations in the World lie under an obligation
' of paying due respect and reverence to Heaven,
' their Rulers Parents, Masters, and Ancestors.
' The Contents of this Paper are exactly true, and
' want no correction at all

The two mention'd *Mandarins* coming out
from the Emperour in consequence to the orders they had reciev'd, intimated this decree in
a Juridical form in the presence of many in the
Inner Court of the Imperial Palace, joyning to the
Inner Hall *Tam Sin Ten*, and one Copy of it was
deliver'd to us, and an other put amongst the Royal Acts.

---

§. III.

*An Account of what ensued upon the Promulgation
of this Decree.*

THis Imperial Decree was reciev'd with great
Applause, many being surpriz'd, that any
Learn'd Men of *Europe* should imagine that those
of *China* did acknowledge, or reverence in
Confucius any thing beyond the dignity of their
Master, and that of a Man eminent for his
Learning; or that they paid him, or the deceas'd
any other then meer civil or political Honour.
Others saying (amongst whom was *Van Tao Hoa*,
a Courtier of eminent Learning) that they Wor-
shiped nothing depriv'd of Life, as the Material
Heavens were: But the Supreme Lord of them,
and

and all things elfe, who fees all, underftands all, and governs all by his Providence : That it was fo evident, that this was the fenfe of the Ancient Philpfophers, above all of *Confuc us* himfelf, that no Man could deny it, without oppofing the krown truth Others exclaiming what each Houfe and Family hath its Mafter, and every Kingdom and Empire then Supreme Lord, who Rules them , and fh all their not be one for the World, who governs it by his Providence, and rules it by his Juftice ? Amongft thefe *S u l io ye,* one of the Members of the Royal College *Hum Lin T'en,* a Man of extraordinary Learning and Wit, and therefore chofen by the Emperour to Tranflate the *Eu ope in Algebra* into *Chinefe.*

The Prefident of the Tribunal of *Mathematicks, Phil pre Grimale'i, Tion s Percyra, Antony Thomas, Joh. Gerbillor,* and the other *Europeans* Petition'd the Emperour in the following manner. 'We your extern Subjects entreat your 'Majefty to Inftruct us in fome points The Lear-'ned Men of *Europe* have heard, that it is cufto-'mary in *China* to reverence *Corren* , other Sa-'crifice to Heaven, and make Offerings to the 'Deceas'd, but do not underftand the meaning of 'thefe Rites : They defire to have an Account of 'it We your Majefty's Subjects believe that '*Corfitius* is Worfhipped in Quality of a Ma-'fter, and not in order to obtain of him Wit, '*Profperity*, or Preferment We lo k upon of-'ferings to be made to the Deceas d, in order on-'ly to teftifie the love the Living bear them, and 'their defire of them, and that it is neither con-'fonant to the *Chinefe* Books, or the fenfe of the
'Learned

'Learned, to beg their Protection: These Cere-
'monies being only Testimonies of the affections
'of the Living towards the Dead, and destin'd
'to renew the memory of them. We add also
'that the Inscriptions usually erected on these
'occasions, are not made use of on account of
'their being persuaded, that the Souls of the
'Dead do reside there, but to supply and stand
'for the persons of the Deceas'd. As for the Sa-
'crifices offer'd to Heaven, we conceive that
'what is Worshipt by them, is not the dark
'blew Heaven, but the Maker and Lord of it, and
'all things else. For *Confucius* says, that the Sa-
'crifices, call'd *K o Xe*, are directed to *Xam*
'*Ti*; or the Supreme Lord of Heaven, who is
'sometimes call'd Heaven, as the Emperour is
'sometimes exprest not by that Name, but by
'these Titles, *beneath the steps of his Throne*;
'*the chief Hall of his Palace*, which expressions,
'tho' different, as to the words, import the self-
'same thing. Your Majesty was heretofore
'pleas'd to honour us with these words in your
'own hand Writing, *Kien Tiè*, i. e. Heaven is
'to be Worshipped, which we understand in the
'sense we have now expounded.

  'We your Majesty's Subjects, not being well
'vers'd in these matters, have Answer'd in this
'manner, but because these Ceremonies belong
'to the Publick Rites of this Nation, we dare
'not rely on our private Authority. We there-
'fore intreat your Majesty to instruct us in them;
'and expect with due reverence and submission
'your Commands. Then follows the Emperours
Answer, as at the end of the second Section.

This

This Relation was sent from Court thro' all the Provinces of the Empire. 'Tis to be observ'd, that in the Translation of it, the word *T* is render'd by Sacrifice, when apply'd to Heaven; and by offering, when apply'd to the Dead. The reason of this difference is the various significations of this Word, which are effectually different in the mention'd cases. As in the Latine Tongue, the word *A o* has a different sense when apply'd to God from what it hath when the Scripture says, that *of o's* Brothers ador'd him Now that this word *T* apply'd to the Dead, doth not import a proper Sacrifice offer'd to them, is evident by the Emperour's Declaration.

§ IV.

The Effects which may be hop'd for from this Declaration.

THE Promulgation of this Imperial Decree may prove very beneficial to this Kingdom For the Emperour's power being very absolute he alone Establishing Laws for his People, and interpreting those which are Establisht, all his decisions relating to the Customs of the Empire, are of great force with his Subjects. In the first place, it will prove a strong Argument against Atheists, and upon account of the repute, this Prince is in for his Learning and Wisdom, a very apt means to wean them from Atheism, and prevail on them to acknowledge the existence of an intelli-

intelligent *Being*, by whom all that is, was Created, and is Govern'd. Frequent experience shews that bare dint of reason can easily prevail on them to acknowledge this Truth, tho' they do not act in consequence to it. Now those same reasons backt by an Authority of this moment, will prove much more forceable 'Tis moreover observable, that many Learn'd Men of this Nation, who in their Discourse and Writing affect to appear Athiests, do not not lash out into these extravagancies upon a full settled Persuasion of the not *Being* of a God, but out of innate Pride of this Nation, which inclines them to distinguish themselves with such Paradoxes 'Tis very clear, that by their comments and glosses on the Ancients, they aim more at the repute of Wits, than at Truth, affecting to reduce all sensible effects and accidents to known natural causes, without recourse to the Supreme Being This attempt is also in vogue among our *European* Philosophers, as far at least as its consistant with Divine Faith. And but to too many slighting the solid Doctrine of the Ancients, and more effectually charm'd with a flash of Wit, and a great Name, than with Truth it self, intrench by affected subtilties on the bounds set by divine Revelation, which when they once pass, transported by an over eager desire of Praise and Credit; tis not at all surprising, that they fall into gross and palpable errors, and promote Atheism both by Discourse and Writing The Emperour of *China* towards the end of the last Year, gave a very exact Character of those his Subjects, who are of this unhappy Temper, saying, ' That the ' Comments and Glosses, by which Moderns
' pretend

' pretended to give a new luſtre to the Writings
' of the Ancients weɪe only now ſubtilties and flo-
' riſhes of Rhetoɪick, by which they affected to
' ſhew their Wɪt, and Eloquence.

Now this ſoɪt of Atheiſm being very rife in
this Empire, and the corruptions and falſe gloſſes on the Ancient Rɪtesof this Nation, rather
takɪng their riſe from an affectation of Subtilty,
and an exceſs of· Pɪɪde, than frcm a belief of
what thoſe Libertɪns advance : By means of this
Decɪee they may eaſily be prevail'd on to renounce
their true or fɪɪgnɪd Atheɪſm. Since its Promulg-
gation thɪo' the Empɪɪe, is an effectual Preaching of the exɪgence of the true God ; which certainly muſt have nc ſmall effect on the minds
of many *Mandeɪɪɪs*, Learn'd Men, and
others, to whoſe knowledge it will be con-
veigh'd by means of the publick News-
Books.

Finally, It will ſtand upon Record, in Quality
of a ſolemn Proteſtation made by the Church of
China, in view of the whole Empire, and approv'd by the Emperour himſtlf, by which the
Chriſtians of thoſe paɪts declare, that in conſe-
quence to the Laws of the Kingdom explicated
by the Emperour himɪelf, they practɪſe the mention'd Rɪtes towaɪds *Confɪcɪɪs* and the Dead ;
not as Religɪous Duties, but in Quality of meer
Civil and Political Ceremonies, ɪenouncing all
ſuperſtɪtɪous Intentɪons and Pɪactɪces, which as
the Emperour decɪaɪes, belong not to their Prɪ-
mɪtɪve Inſtitutɪon, but have inſenſibly crept in
bɪ lenɪth of tɪɪe, and the blindneſs and propen-
ſioɪ of Mankɪɪd to Idolatɪy

§. V.

§. V.

Teftimonies of many Eminent for their Dignities and Learning in the Chinefe *Empire, agreeing with the Emperour's Decree in Relation to the fenfe and meaning of the Rites in Queftion.*

THis clear and diftinct Declaration of the Emperour ought in reafon to be look'd upon as fufficient to evince, that the *Chinefe* Rites, which are the fubject of the prefent Difpute, are only Civil Duties, for it belongs to him alone in quality of Supreme Legiflator, and Interpreter of the Laws of the Empire to determine the fenfe and meaning of them : And his prefent Declaration feems to leave no further doubt concerning that point. However for a further clearing of this Truth, and leaft any thing fhould feem wanting on our part, it was thought expedient to know their Sentiment concerning thefe cuftoms, who are at prefent in greateft repute in this Empire, as well on account of their great Dignities, as their eminent skill in the *Chinefe* Literature. And to the end thefe Authentical Teftimonies may not be queftion'd in after times ; they are kept in Archives of the College of *Pekin* ; partly Sign'd and Seal'd by thofe who gave them ; partly made good by the authentical Teftimonies of thofe who reciev'd them by word of mouth only ; when it was not judg'd expedient to demand them in Writing

C   from

from perfons of that eminent Dignity and Character, whom they confulted.

The firft fhall be of a Prince in great repute in this Court, the prefent Emperours Younger Brother, who is now about Forty Years Old; and who as being neither addicted to Hunting, nor the other Entertainments, which Princes generally delight in, has imploy'd his time in Reading, and Studies. One of the Fathers went to pay his refpects to him on the Second day of *May*, 1701, in order to know his fentiment concerning the *Chinefe* Rites. Being admitted to Audience, and order'd to fit down, the Prince's Four Sons ftanding over againft their Father. After feveral Queftions propos'd by the Prince relating to different matters, and his obliging, fhewing the Father a Map of the World, Accuratly and Ingenioufly drawn on a Fann by the Prince himfelf: The Father offer'd to his perufal an Expofition of the *Chinefe* Rites in the *Tartar* Tongue, and felf-fame words, it had been prefented to the Emperour. The Prince Read it attentively, and approv'd of it. And then added, That the Ancient *Chinefe* were free from all fuperftitious Worfhip, which in procefs of time had crept in by degrees; that they Ador'd only *Xam Ti*, or the Supreme, and Living Lord of Heaven; that by that Name, as alfo by the word *Heaven* they meant the fame Creator, and Governor of the Univerfe, whom Chriftians Ador'd under the Name of the Lord of Heaven, and that to him alone they offer'd Sacrifice. He gave great encomiums of Father *Riccius* his Books, which Treat of the Exiftence of God: He had reciev'd them fome few Months before in

the

the *Tartar* Language, and afterwards procur'd them in *Chinese*. These same Books were also highly prais'd by the presumptive Heir of the Empire in presence of several Fathers of the Society. Now in these Books, F. *Rucius* undertakes to prove by Texes of the *Chinese* Authors, that the Ancient *Chinese* by *Xam Ti* meant, and Ador'd not the Material Heavens, but the True God and Lord of Heaven and Earth.

The Emperour further added, That the Moral Precepts of *Confucius* agreed with those the Christian Law prescrib'd, in which he is well verst: That this Philosopher only Explain'd those which related to this Life, without mentioning that which is to follow; because he found it so difficult a task to gain belief to what he Taught, in relation to what is sensible, and present, that he thought Men would never be prevail'd with, to assent to what concern'd things which did not fall under their senses. Finally, after many Questions concerning Angels, Devils, separate Souls, Prayers for the Dead, and other matters belonging to Religion; concerning which he Heard, the Father Discourse near two hours, his Sons standing all the while, he dismiss'd him with as obliging Testimonies, as he had reciev'd him with Honour.

The second Testimony shall be that we had from the Illustrious *So Sin Lao Ye*, who was for Ten Years *Colao*, or first Minister of the Empire, then President of the Tribunal of Rites, and at present Commands the Emperour's Guards, and is one of his Chief Counsellers. This is he, who was Chosen in the Year 92, of the last Age, to prevail upon the Tribunals of Rites, and the *Co-*

lao's

rio's to grant by a publick Edict free Liberty to the Christian Religion, towards which he was well affected; and he manag'd the business so dexterously, that he obtain'd it.

This Eminent Man being consulted on the First of April, 1701, by two of the Society concerning the meaning of the *Chinese* Rites, gave this Answer. 'I will very willingly declare to you 'the Truth of this business, and what has always 'been the sense of the wisest Men among 'us *Confucius* was a Man of Eminent Probity, 'and Learning, he has left us excellent Precepts 'for the Regulating our Lives, the Governing our 'Families, and the Empire it self, and on that 'account he is Honour'd, as a Man of Exemplar 'Probity and Eminent Wisdom: He neither was 'in himself, nor is acknowledg'd by us to be 'more than Man. The Worship which is Paid 'him, and the Ceremonies us'd in it, are of a dif- 'ferent nature from those, by which Spirits and 'Idols are Worship'd. Neither do we by these 'Ceremonies, which are only Testimonies of our 'Respect and Gratitude towards our Master, ei- 'ther ask, or hope any help or happiness from him. Being ask'd, if their were not some, who be- liev'd that the Soul of *Confucius* did Reside, or at least Descend down to the Inscriptions, before which these Rites were perform'd; he rejected this fancy very warmly, and said with some In- dignation. 'For be it from the grave Doctrine 'to admit of such manners of speaking; to be 'met with only amongst the Illiterate, and Cor- 'rupters of the *Chinese* Laws, or of such Practices 'no ways agreeable to the sense and apprehensi- 'on of Wise Men.

Then

Then being entreated to deliver his Opinion concerning the Ceremonies us'd towards the Dead. He Answer'd, 'That they were not Wor-'shiped by the Understanding part of the Na-'tion as Idols, and Spirits, but Honour'd in a 'Civil and Political way; that nothing was ei-'ther askt, or hop'd for from them, that the 'sole and only end of all the Solemn Rites us'd 'on such occasions, as frequent inclinations of 'the Body, presenting of Meats, burning of 'Perfumes, and other Offerings; was, that by 'these exteriour Ceremonies, their Posterity 'might express their Love, and gratitude to them, 'and longing desire of them, as if they were really 'present to recieve these Testimonies of their 'Love, and Respect, and that the Inscriptions, 'before which these Ceremonies were perform'd, 'were plac'd there on no other account. He moreover added, 'That what he had said con-'cerning the Honours paid to *Confucius*, could 'neither be Oppos'd or Question'd by any Man, 'unless he betray'd his Ignorance, and was guilty 'of Heresy, against the Doctrine of the Lear-'ned.

Finally, being desir'd to let us understand what was the genuine meaning of *Xin Ti*, and Heaven, concerning whose Worship, and Invocation the Learned of *China*, treat so fusely: He said, 'The Learned Men of *China*, when 'they Treat of the Worship, and Invocation of 'Heaven, do not mean by the word *Tien*, the Ma-'terial and Visible Heaven, but *Xam Ti*, or the 'Supreme Lord of Heaven, Creator of all Things, 'the Fountain of all Good, and Master of the 'Universe, who Sees, Hears, and Governs all

Things

'Things, in a word the self-same, whom we
Christians Adore under the Name of *Tien Chu*,
or Lord of Heaven. Then he added, 'That
' when he was sent by the Emperour's Command
' to prevail in the Tribunal of Rites, and the
' *Colco's* to grant a free Liberty for the Exer-
' cife of Christian Religion, from which
' seve al were Averse; he infilted chiefly on
' this Reason; to bring them over to it.
' That we Adore the same Lord, which *Ch na*
' had Worshipt from time out of mind, and that
' it was evident that the Supreme Lord of all
' Things was the self-same, whom we *Fu opeans*
' call'd *Tien Chu*, whom their Philosophers and
' Wise Men Ador'd under the Name of *Tien*,
' and *Xam Ti*.

Now this same Eminent Person having frequently been near the Emperour's Person, when
he offer'd Sacrifice in the Temples, *Tien Tw*,
and *Ti Tew*, that are Dedicated to Heaven and
Earth; or to speak more properly, to the Supreme Lord of both; as it appears very evident
ly by the Inscriptions Grav'd on their Frontif-
pieces; and that which is exprefs'd, when Sacrifice is offer'd, which shall be mention'd in their
due place; and having been also deputed by the
Emperour to offer Sacrifice in his Name, in the
Temples mention'd · We entreated him to give us
some account of these Temples, and Sacrifices. In
these Temples, and Sacrifices, says he, ' There
' is nothing that favours of Superstition, no-
' thing that borders on Idolatry; there is neither
' Statue, nor Painted Image; nothing in fine but
' this Inscription, *Xam Ti*, or Supreme Lord of
' Heaven. Neither is any thing contain'd in the
' Solemn Invocation Read, a loud in the Emper-
' our s

' our's Name, whilst he Sacrifices, besides a Pray-
' er, and Addressed to the Supreme Lord of Hea-
' ven, containing a demand of all such things, as
' seem necessary for the publick Happiness, and
' Tranquillity of the Empire.

Upon this concluding of his Discourse, the
Fathers offer'd to his perusal the above mention'd
Exposition of the *Chinese* Rites, which had been
presented to the Emperour, which he perused,
and said to each Article contain'd in it; 'This is
' exactly so, this agrees perfectly with what I
' told you, this is the Genuine sense of the *Chi-*
' *nese* Rites very accuratly exprest.

The Third Testimony shall be, that which we
had from *Min Lio Ye*, a Man no ways Inferior,
either in Dignity or Authority, and as well affected towards its Preachers, as his Colleague,
whom we spoak of last. He was first Colao, or
Minister of the Empire for Fifteen Years; at
present he is of the Emperour's Council, and one
of the chief Men at Court. In his younger
Years, on account of his eminent skill in the
Chinese and *Tartar* Tongues; he was made Pre-
fect of the Royal Library by the Emperour *Xum
Chi*, and imploy'd in Translating the *Chinese*
Books into *Tartar*. So that by reason of the
great Repute he is in at Court, on account of
his eminent Learning, and great Authority, he is
known and respected thro' the whole extent of
the Empire.

Two of the Fathers went on the 21th of
April, 1701, to know his sentiment concerning
the custom'd Honours paid to Heaven, *Confucius*, and the Dead. His Answers agreed perfectly
with those of his Colleague, and differ'd only in

some

some few words He frequently inculcated, that the Learned did not acknowledge the least shadow of Divinity, or any power more than Humane in *Confucius*, or the Dead, that they neither pretended, or hop'd any thing from them. He was surpriz'd to hear that some in *Europe* imagin'd, that the Learn'd *Chinese* Worshiped *Confucius*, or the Dead, as Idols, and Spirits, which they conciev'd endow'd with Power to benefit them, and could not forbear laughing at their simplicity, and reproaching it to them, as highly Injurious to the Wisdom of the *Chinese*. He further added, ‘ That the publick Buildings ‘ Erected to *Confucius*, and their deceas'd Ancestors, were only Testimonies of their gratitude and respect towards them, towards *Confucius* in Quality of their Master ; on account of ‘ his having restor'd the Precepts necessary to ‘ live up to the light of Reason, and establish ‘ excellent Rules for the Government of the Empire, towards their Ancestors, on the account ‘ of having reciev'd from them their Life and E‘ ducation. He repeated over and over again, ‘ That no Man skill'd in the great Doctrine, could ‘ say, or believe, that the Souls of *Confucius*, or ‘ the Dead, resided in, or descended down to ‘ the Inscriptions *Xin Guey*, before which these ‘ Ceremonies were perform'd ; that these ‘ were placed there on no other design, but to ‘ stand for, and supply the place of the Dead, ‘ and raise a more lively remembrance of ‘ them.

His Answers to our Questions concerning the words *Tien*, and *Xam Ti*, agreed perfectly with those his Companion had given *viz.* ¡The Learn'd *Chinese* had from time out of mind, meant and

Wor-

Worſhip'd under thoſe Names, the Supreme Lord of Heaven, and Earth, endow'd with underſtanding, and no ways different from the true God, whom we Chriſtians call *Tien Chu*, and whom he had lately Ador'd in our Church Then he told us, that in the Perſecution, which was rais'd by *Yam Quam Sien* in the Year 1664, in which he himſelf was concern'd, and an Eye-Witneſs of what paſs'd ; a great Aſſembly of the Princes, and chief Perſons of the Empire were of the ſame Opinion, and had certainly pronounc'd in favour of the Chriſtian Religion, had not this Impious Accuſer of the Chriſtians, ſeeing how ill he was like to ſucceed, produc'd an Image of Chriſt Crucify'd, which he ſaid the Chriſtians Ador'd, as Supreme Lord of all things; which in this Aſſembly of *Gentils*, who know little of the Chriſtian Religion, rais'd a ſuſpicion againſt it, as favouring of Superſtition, and dangerous Novelty.   On this occaſion it will not be unſeaſonable to remark ; how notoriouſly the Society was defam'd by ſome at *Rome*, who charg'd it with concealing the Miſtery of Chriſt Crucify d : Since this Accuſer produc'd at that time againſt it, as a known and publick Crime, a Picture of Chriſt Crucify'd, which he had taken out of our Books, and caus'd to be Grav'd, and ſpread abroad, in order to cover us with ſhame and confuſion.

Being finally conſulted about the Rites and Sacrifices us'd in the Temples *Tien Ti*, and *Ti Tan*; at which he had frequently aſſiſted near the Emperour's perſon , and ſometimes offer'd in his name : His Anſwer agreed with thoſe of the preſent Teſtimonies, *viz.* that in theſe

two

two Temples, tho' different as to place and name, the same Supreme Lord of Heaven and Earth was Ador d , that the difference of place and building of, these Temples, was only introduc'd by the Emperour *Hia Cin* of the Family *Tai Mim*, who began his Reign in 1522, before whom there was only one *Tian Tan* (that is in *Pekin* under that Family) in which *Xam Ti*, or the Supreme Lord of Heaven and Earth, Sun, Moon, and Stars, and all things else was Ador d

This Discourse being ended, the Emperour's Declaration was offer'd him; after he had attentively perus'd it; you see, says he, how exactly I have explicated to you the true sense of these Rites; and how, what I said agrees with this Declaration; it never enter'd into the head of the Learned, and well verst in the great Doctrine, to imagine that *Confucius*, or the Dead had any power to bestow benefits on us, or to demand, or hope any thing from them, or that their Souls were really present in the Inscriptions hung up on such occasions; who is the Author of these Dreams? These Rites and Ceremonies were instituted to no other end, than to express our respect and gratitude towards the Dead, and Absent; as tho' they were present. This is the genuine sense of our Books, where the Text has not *Ti Ti*, that is, *that they are present*; but *Pisfue adali*, as if they were present; for he spoak in the *Tartar*, and not in the *Chinese* Tongue.

The Fourth Testimony of this Truth shall be, that we reciev d from *Y Stanha*, who has now for Fourteen Years been Colao, or first
Minister :

Minister : This Man was Son to a common
Souldier, but so successful in his Studies, that
he is risen by degrees from the lowest degree
of Magistrature, to the Supreme, which he
performs with great Applause. He is so
much valued by the Emperour, that tho' his
great Age hath frequently oblig'd him to Petition his discharge, he has never been able to obtain it. This eminent Man, who for several
Years was President of the Tribunal of Rites,
was on the 28th of *May* 1701, desir'd by two
Fathers to deliver his own, and the Learned
mens sense concerning the Rites in Question.
First he desir'd to be inform'd on what account
this Question was put to him He was told,
that twas on no other motive, than in order to
have a right understanding of them from him ;
than whom, the whole Empire scarce furnisht
any man more skilful in them. Since from his
tender Age he had been addicted to Studies, and
without any help, than that of his Learning,
and dexterity in managing business ; he had
pass'd thro' all the different degrees of Magistrature, and finally had attain'd that of chief
Minister : That some doubts had been started
in *Europe* concerning the meaning of these
Ceremonies, whither they desir'd to send a
true account of them Having heard that this
was the occasion of his being consulted, he
said, those Ceremonies were only us'd as
Testimonies of gratitude and respect ; and added no more. Then the Fathers presented him the
exposition of those Rites, which had been offer'd to the Emperour, but without any mention of the Answer they had reciev'd from him :
They further added, that by *Tien*, or *Xam Ti*,
it

it was not meant, that the Learn'd Ador'd the
Material Heavens; but a spiritual Being endow'd
with reason and understanding, to whom it be
long'd to reward Good, and punish Evil. He
Read this Exposition over and over, made some
pause, and consider'd with most attention what
was said concerning the understanding of this
Supreme Being, and the rewarding good, and
punishing Evil: Then giving the Writing back
to the Fathers, he said, it's so as you have Explicated it · You have explain'd these Rites very clearly, and in their true sense and meaning.
Tho' this Answer seem'd sufficient, as to all contain'd in that Exposition ; notwithstanding
they inquir'd further, if any thing more than
Humane was believ'd to be in *Confucius*, or the
Dead ? If any thing was desir'd, or hop'd for
from them ? If the Learn'd believ'd that the
Soul of *Confucius*, or the Dead, resided in the
Inscriptions expos'd on those occasions, or descended down to them, or were fed with the
Fumes of those Meats which were offer'd ? He
rejected these fancies with a smile, and said, 'how
'can they believe such things? And if any Ad-
'dress'd their Prayers to them, would they there-
'fore obtain what they desir'd ? All our Cere-
'monies are only Testimonies of gratitude to-
'wards the Master of the Empire, and those
'from whom we reciev'd our lives This was
the Answer given by this Colao, a Man of
great Authority, and the first who Subscrib'd
the Decree, by which, Liberty was granted to
the Christian Religion.

The

The Fifth Teſtimony ſhall be that, which on account of his Nobility and Authority who gave it, might deſerve the firſt place, who had it from the Succeſſour of *Confucius*, who is at preſent head of the Family, which has for many Years poſſeſs'd a large Principality in the Province *Xam Tum*, where the Philoſophers Sepulcher is, and where his Deſcendents reſide in the Ancient Seat of their Family. Now this Man muſt be well skill'd in the Honours done to *Confucius*, Living on the place where the Emperours themſelves perform them to him. Neither can he in reaſon be ſuſpected to be wanting in his endeavours to keep them up to their hight, ſince the reſpects paid to the chief perſon of his Family, do in no ſmall meaſure redound to his Credit.

On his coming to Court this Year on the Emperour's Birth-Day, two Fathres ask'd his Opinion of the Expoſition of the *Chineſe* Rites, which had been preſented to the Emperour: After he had perus'd it, he Anſwer'd by a Writing Sign'd and Seal'd by him in theſe words I have ſeen your Anſwer to the *Europears* concerning the Rites of this Kingdom, *viz*. That *Confucius* is Honour'd on account of his Doctrine, and not in order to obtain Proſperity or Protection from him: 'Tis truly ſo; you have Alledg'd the true motive of theſe Rites

The Sixth Teſtimony we had from the *Chineſe* Colao *Vam bi*, a Man famous thro' the Empire for his Learning and Prudence; and who for this Twenty Years has been Colao; being as't his Opinion of the Rites

in Queſtion ; he Anſwer'd by a Writing Sign'd
and Seal'd by him in theſe terms. 'I have ſeen
'your Writing expoſing the *Chineſe* Rites ; you
'have clearly and diſtinctly laid open the true
'and genuine ſenſe, in which the Learn'd and
'Wiſe *Chineſe* Worſhip Heaven, their Deceas'd
'Anceſtors, and their Maſter. The Decree
which the Emperour has Publiſht according to
the Laws of the Empire, concerning this Expoſition of them, agrees perfectly with the
Doctrine of *Confucius*.

The Seventh Teſtimony was given by an
other *Chineſe*, Famous for his Learning, Nam'd
Cham Ym : He for many Years Taught the Emperour and his Children the *Chineſe* Tongue ;
was for many more Preſident of the Tribunal of
Rites, and has now been for ſome Years Colao.
Being deſir'd to give his Opinion of our Expoſition of the *Chineſe* Rites ; he return'd this
Anſwer, Sign'd and Seal'd by him. 'I have
'ſeen a Copy of a Letter, which the *Europeans*
'reſiding here have Written to their Friends
'there ; and I obſerv'd in it a clear and true
'Expoſition of the motives, which induc'd us
'to offer Sacrifices to Heaven, and uſe thoſe Ce-
'remonies, by which we Honour Men eminent
'for their Virtue ; and our Deceas'd Anceſtors ;
'and hence I perceiv'd the ſaid *Europeans* ſo well
'verſt in our *Claſſick* Authors , that they have
'been able to diſtinguiſh Truth from Error,
'and attain the moſt abſtruſe and ſublime ſenſe
'of them. Nay their Sentiment perfectly a-
'grees with the Rites and Practices preſcrib'd
'by our moſt wiſe Anceſtors. So for the en-
tire ſatisfaction of thoſe to whom they Write ;

'tis

'tis only neceffary to defire them to Read o-
ver their Anfwer approv'd by the Emperour;
for that contains all that can in reafon be
defir'd, for the peifect underftanding of thefe
Rites and Ceremonies.

The Eighth Teftimony was given by a Man,
who may in reafon be lookt on, as the Learned'ft
Man in the Empire, call'd *Han*, he is at prefent
Prefident of the Tribunal, Compos'd of the
chief Doctors of this Kingdom, chofen by the
Emperour himfelf, after a very rigorous examine.
This Tribunal is call'd *Ham Lin Yuen*, and is of
very great Authority in this Empire. He is alfo
Prefident of the Tribunal of the Rites, and Famous for his Learning. This eminent Man having perus'd the Expofition of the *Chinefe*
Rites, which had been prefented to the Emperour, in order to be fent into *Europe*, gave his
fenfe of it, in a Writing Sign'd and Seal'd by
him in thefe words ' They have attain'd the
' true and genuine fenfe of the chief Heads of
' the *Chinefe* Doctrine, relating to the Worfhip
' of *Xam Ti*, and the Ceremonies by which we Ho-
' nour our Deceas'd Anceftors, and our Mafter, for
' on the perufal of the Declaration of them,
' which they fend to their Friends in *Europe* : I
' obferv'd it to agree perfectly with the Doctrine
' of our Anceftors, and the fublime and excellent
' fenfe of our *Claffick* Books. Some other Doc-
tois of this fame Supreme Tribunal, to whom
belongs all that relates to Learning, and the In-
teipietation of their Claffical Authors have
given the fame, or equivalent Teftimonies under
their Hands and Seals.

The

The Ninth Teſtimony we had from him who in the Tribunal of Rites, is next in Dignity to the Preſident, and of great Authority among the Doctors, who are Members of it: His Name is *Sun*; he is at preſent Keeper of the Royal Library, and Preſident of the Tribunal, to which the Regulating and Interpreting of the Ceremonies relating to *Confucius*, doth appertain. One of the Society going on the Firſt of the Third Moon of this Year 1701, into the Hall of the great Seminary of *Confucius* Erected at *Pekin*, call'd *Gue cu Kien*, which is the chief of all Erected thro' this Empire, to this Philoſopher: He met there the Preſident of the place, and Ceremonies uſually perform'd towards *Confucius*, call'd *Sin Lao Ye*; and being askt by him on what account he came; he Anſwer'd, ' That ' he came thither on purpoſe to be inform'd by ' him, who was ſo well verſt in the *Chineſe* Rites, ' and Preſident of that place: What was the ' ſenſe of the Learn'd *Chineſe* concerning the ' Worſhip of Heaven, *Confucius*, and their An- ' ceſtors, and then preſented him a Writing a- greeing with that which had been offer'd to the Emperour, but without making any mention of that Prince's Approbation of it. The Preſident Read it attentively, and weighed every word and ſyllable, and approv'd all that was contain'd in it, declaring it to agree perfectly with the ſenſe of the Learn'd But he prais'd nothing more than the laſt Paragraf, which treated of the Worſhip of Heaven, and above all, ſome words which were added, and attributed to *Xam Ti*, Supreme Intelligence.

The

The Tenth and Laſt ſhall be the Teſtimony we had from a venerable Old Man, not ſo much to be valu'd for his great dignities, as on account of his Eminent Learning, which render'd him both venerable to the *Tartars*, and *Chineſe*. His Name was *Li*, he had been for ſeveral Years imploy'd by the Emperour, in compounding ſeveral Treatiſes, as well in the *Tartar*, as *Chineſe* Tongue, concerning different matters, but chiefly relating to the different Sects, which are in this Empire, as alſo in doing into theſe two Languages (both which he poſſeſt in perfection) ſeveral Books relating to our *European* Sciences. He had formerly done out of *Chineſe* into *Tartu*, Father *Matthew Riccius*'s Books concerning the exiſtence of God, and ſeveral others, which have been Printed much to the Publick good. This Learned Man ſo eminent for his knowledge of the *Chineſe* Antiquities, that none ſurpaſs'd him in it, being heretofore askt by one of the Society (for he has been dead ſome Years) what he thought of the mention'd Books, and their Author He Anſwer'd ingeniouſly, ‘ That they contain'd the ‘ Doctrine of the Ancient *Chineſe*, in relation ‘ to the Worſhip of Heaven, and *Xam Ti*, and ‘ ſhew'd its perfect Conformity as to thoſe points ‘ with the Chriſtian Religion. He added, He ‘ could not ſufficiently admire how it was poſſi- ‘ ble for Father *Riccius* to penetrate the abſtruſe ‘ and hidden ſenſe of their Canonical Books, ‘ and for a ſtranger to give light by his piercing ‘ Wit, to thoſe Truths, which had for many Years ‘ ſeem'd obſcure to their greateſt Doctors For ‘ he has, ſays he, demonſtrated that the Belief

D
‘and

'and Worſhip of the true God, was the firſt
'and chief point of Wiſdom amongſt the An-
'cient *Chineſe*; and that ſo clearly, that the ve-
'ry pretenders to Learning may with much
'eaſe and evidence diſcover this important Truth
'in his Books   The ſame perſon had done out of
Chineſe into the *Tartar* Tongue, Father *Alenus*
his Treatiſe of the true Origen of all things;
which Tranſlation is extent in Print. He ſaid
this Father was ſomewhat inferiour to the former, as to the knowledge of the *Chineſe* Antiquities, but that for elegance and purity of his
ſtile in that Tongue, he might be rankt with the
moſt famous Orators and Philoſophers of that
Nation, not excepting the Ancients themſelves.
He who heard theſe things from this great Man,
both left under-Oath the Truth of what is here
ſet down, and his Teſtimony is kept at *Pekin.*

Many other Teſtimonies of Men eminent for
their Dignities and Learning might be added to
theſe, and many more might have been procur'd
from thoſe who are Learn'd Men, but of an inferiour rank; but becauſe a too diligent enquiry after many Mens Opinions, might create
ſome ſuſpition, and come to the Emperour's
ears, who would not at all be pleas'd, that we
ſhould not reſt ſatisfy'd with this Decree:
We thought it convenient to ſuperſeed all farther enquiry, by means of which it would have
been eaſy, if any ways neceſſary, to have procur'd innumerable other Teſtimonies, which
would all agree in the ſame Explication of the
Chineſe Rites and Ceremonies.

We

We could add to thefe feveral Teftimonies
of fome of more Ancient ftanding; as that of
Doctor *Paul*, who by means of more Ancient
ftanding, and his eminent Learning arriv'd to
the Dignity of Colao, and thofe of feveral o-
ther Chriftians, whofe eminent Science has
rais'd them to great Dignities, whofe Authority
muft certainly be more valuable, than of Ten
unknown Chriftians, who were cited at *Rome*,
in the Year 1645, againft the opinion of the
Society But we muft not omit here that the
Authentick Teftimony of the Famous Colao *Ye*,
taken out of the Archive of *Pekin* College, and
related in a Letter Written by Father *Alenus*
in *Ham Cheu*, the Third of *February* 1625, in
which he gives the following Relation, Tra-
vailing by Water with the Colao *Ye*, and fpeaking to him conceining the Divine Law , he faid,
we alfo acknowledge one God, Lord of the U-
niverfe, who Rewards the Good, and Punifhes
the Evil, but under a different name. For you
call him *Tien Chu*, that is, Lord of Heaven,
which way of fpeaking is no fmall prejudice to
you, making you pafs for Men of a New and
evil Sect; and all this happens, becaufe you do
not give him the fame name we do. Why therefore do you not ufe the terms *Tien*, and *Xam Ti*,
to fignifie the true God ? By that means you
would avoid all fufpicion of Novelty; and if
you thought it neceffary, you might by a further
explication limit more particularly the fenfe of
thefe words, to what you defir'd, and defign'd
to fignify by them. He faid afterwards, we
reafon upon a Parity drawn from our Bodies,
in which there is a Spirit or Soul, who governs

D 2   it,

it, and without which, it can neither suſtain it ſelf, or act, whence we infer, that there muſt be in the World, a Supreme Lord, who governs it, and directs all things to his deſign'd end, in this we agree perfectly with you, this was the diſcourſe of this Colao, famous in his time for his Learning, who cheriſhed and valued highly the Chriſtian Doctrine, and its Preachers, tho' he was not ſo happy, as to embrace it himſelf.

---

§ VI.

Certain Proofs of the Worſhip due to God, in this preſent Tradition.

THere are yet extant in this Empire, ma-ny clear and evident proofs of its know-ledge of the true God, which agrees perfectly with the action and Territories of the Emperour, and the other matters of it. We thought conven-ient to place them in this place under the name of Tradition, as having from time out of mind, been conveyed from hand to hand down to this preſent Age. Amongſt theſe, the firſt place is due to what occurs in two Temples Erected at Pekin, in the Emperours and Empires name. The one is called Tun Tan, the o-ther Ti Tan. One of the Society by the Em-perours Authority, aſſiſted on ſet purpoſe theſe Temples, ſcarce known even to the Learn'd them-ſelves of this Nation, who are of an inferiour

rank,

rank. He was reciev'd at the entrance by Six *Mandarins*, Keepers of the place, and well acquainted with all things relating to the Temples, and being honourably led into them, he view'd and search'd at leasure into all things that concern either the Buildings, or the Rites observ'd there, insomuch, that he omitted nothing which might help to the perfect knowledge of the Ceremonies perform'd there, or the Plain, or Icnography of the Building. We shall at present cull out of many things he observ'd, and which may one day appear at length, some few which belong to the matter in hand, which shall be compris'd under the three following Heads; the first of which shall contain an account of the object to which the Sacrifices offer'd here are directed, the second relate to the matter and form of these Sacrifices, and the third treat of the Person who Sacrifices there, and of the Rites and Ceremonies he uses. We shall begin with the *Tien Tan*, as being far the most Ancient.

Of the Temple Tien Tan.

In the first place, what is Ador'd in this Temple, hath not the least shadow of an Idol in it. There is neither Statue nor Image, nor any resemblance of any thing whatsoever. In both the *Northern* and *Southern* Temple there is nothing, but an Inscription upon a moveable Table in the *Chinese* and *Tartar* Tongues, and neat Letters of Gold. The *Chinese* Characters are *Hoam Tien Xam Ti*, to which these three *Tartar* words, correspond *Terghi ab Cai Han*; that is word for word, *The High and Supreme Lord of Heaven.*

On the front of the *Southern* Temple, there is this *Chinese* Inscription; *Hoam Kium yu*, done thus into *Tartar, Ab Cai Humm ordo*: That is the Temple of the Supreme Lord of Heaven. Finally, the *Chinese* Inscription on the *Northern* front, is, *Hoam Kien Tien*, the Hall of the Supreme Lord of Heaven, for the *Tartars* Translate it thus, *Ab Cai Hamm Ter.*

On this occasion, the Reader not well verst in the affairs of *China*, is defir'd to observe, that these *Tartar* Translations of the Ancient *Chinese* Inscriptions, fo very remote from any dubious, or fuperftitious fenfe, were perform'd by Men eminently skill'd in both thefe Languages, and after a long Confultation, had in order to difcover the true fenfe and meaning of the *Chinese* Empire, and were by the late Emperour, and the Sovereign Tribunals judg'd to bear the fame fenfe with the *Chinese* Characters, and order'd to be added to them; tho' the *Chinese* Infcriptions bear a full and compleat fenfe, and in the Opinion of many, exprefs the fame thing with yet more energy. For befides the four laft Characters fignifying by their Primitive Inftitution, the Supreme Emperour. The firft Character *Hoam*, which in common acception imports the fame; hath moreover by Virtue of the *Hieroglyphick* Characters which Compofe it, a very intenfe fignification of abfolute Dominion over all things. For it is made up of the Letter *Pe*, which fignifies a Hundred, which in their Language is equivalent to *All* in ours, and the Letter *Vam*, which signifies Kings. Whence the *Chinese*, who are the most Proud of Men, have sometimes thro' Flattery still'd their Emperour *Hoam*. Hence it is evident that the *Chinese* Inscriptions are not unbecoming the Majesty of our God, who is still'd in Scripture, the Heavenly King, and Lord of Lords.

Now these terms of Heavenly King, Supreme Lord, and the like, being very usual in common Discourse, and as *Tertulian* discourses concerning the word *God*, being known to every Mans Conscience, and not owing their Institution to the Temples of Idols, or the Schools of Philosophy, they may be certainly of great use, as being very apt to raise in the minds of those who hear them, either here or any where else, an apprehension of a Supreme and Living Being: who governs all things according to his Pleasure. Those few, who in *China*, as also in *Europe*, endeavour by silly quirks, and forc'd glosses on evident Texts to bear down this common sentiment of Mankind, are indeed valued by their followers, as great Wits, but they will be always lookt upon by the sober and thinking part of the World, as Men, who voluntarily shut their Eyes to avoid seeing the clear and evident light of this Truth.

What concerns the Victims and Solemnities of the Sacrifices usually offer'd in these Temples, may be compris'd in these few words, *viz.* That they have a very great Affinity with these which were in use under the Law of Nature;

and

and that of *Moyses* For in the first place, they are not sullied with any of those Crimes, which all our Historie observe, to have accompany'd the *Pagan* Sacrifices Here is no spilling of Humane Blood, nothing obscene, no momery, all that is practis'd is highly respectful and decent Some Victims are us'd here as under the Old Law, and chiefly Bulls and Oxen. They have also different sorts of Sacrifices, some Expiatory, others Propitiatory; others in Thanksgiving; others still'd Emperial, offer'd for the obtaining of new Favours. *V. G.* the *Tien Tan* hath within its enclosure a noble Temple, call'd *K. a. T.*, where Sacrifice is offer'd for the obtaining Corn necessary for the sustinance of the People. Amongst these Sacrifices those are the chief, which have the Quality of Holocausts, in which the Victim, *viz.* a young Bull well Fatted, and particularly chosen, is Burnt, and that upon a square Altar made hallow beneath, with a Grate, in its size, situation, and dimensions, scarce different from that us'd by the Jews. The same resemblance is also to be found between the Altar, on which the *Chinese* do offer and burn Perfumes In their ways of Slaughtering their Victims, sometimes cutting them in pieces, or taking out the Entrals, and heaping them on a Pile of wood and sometimes boyling the Flesh, and offering a kind of Banket of it, and other times Tables before the Sacred name of God, which practice is observ'd by Interpreters to have been us'd in the Sacrifices of the old Law Amongst others he notes, that their Sacrifice was a kind of Banket, offer'd to God, which The conduct or is deputed to act in his name.

name. The defign'd Brevity of this Treatife permits us not to inftance all the cautions which are
obferv'd, and the Laws which are Eftablifht in
relation to the choife of the Victims to be Offer'd, and the Minifters deputed to keep this
Temple. All Beafts aie rejected, which are either hurt, maim'd, or obnoxious to any of the
defects mention'd in the 22th of *Leviticus*; and
thofe which aie admit_ed into the Paftures, allot-
ted for the Beafts defign'd for the Sacrifices, are
nourifh'd, wafh'd, and fatned, with fingular
caie and diligence. Gieater caution is us'd in
choofing thofe who feive in this Temple. They
are always men of unfpotted Fame and integrity,
and no common Learning, chofen fiom among
the moft confiderable *Mandeims*; not only they
aie uncapable of this employ, who have been
condemn'd in publick Courts of Juftice, found
guilty of any Ciime, or fuffer'd any publick
Punifhment, but thofe alfo, who have the mif-
foitune to be liable to any natural defect.

At the Four Seafons of the Year, when Sacrifices aie to be offei'd, an Univeifal Thiee days
Faft is commanded, confifting in Abftinence fiom
Flefh and Wine, Women, Comedies, and the
Piofecution of all Litigeous Caufes, and affaiis.
On this account the *Mandeims* aie oblig'd to lie
out of their own Houfes in the publick [Tribu-
nals: Nay the Empeiour himfelf leaves his Palace, and ietiies into the *Chay Crm*, or Hall of
Penance, built within the Piecincts of the Temple; whcre in folitude he attends to himfelf a-
lone, and, as they fay, endeavouis to perfect
himfelf by a diligent examine of his Actions,
and a fiim puipofe of amendmeet. In order

to

to reduce all the *Manderins* to the same practise.
A Table is hung up during these Three days, in the
publick Tribunals, bearing this Inscription *The
Kingdom has its Law : There is a Spirit, who
sees those, who observe it, and who transgress
it.* So far were the Ancient *Chinese* perswaded, that
Men might be prevail'd upon, by the apprehension of a Spirit, that did see, and know all
things; to forbear transgressing the Laws Establisht, in relation to the Sacrifices to be offer'd
to him.

Whence this great resemblance of the Rites of
this Empire, with those of the old Law, took its
rise; and why this so uncommon preparation,
both of body and mind, was order'd to preceed
the Sacrifices to be offer'd to the Supreme Lord
of the Universe, we leave others to determine.
But we are inclin'd to believe, that the concur-
rance of all these observances, which were instituted many Ages ago; will convince any Man
Read in Antiquity : That the *Chinese* Monarchy
during its first Ages, enjoy'd a clear knowledge
of the true God; and that these customs flow
from a pure fountain : Since the Intervening,
superstitions, which from time to time
have obscur'd this Light, could never prevail so far, as to extinguish it, or hinder
succeeding Princes of greater Wisdom, from re-
storing it in some measure to its first Lustre
All that we pretend at present, is barely to re-
present things as we find them, and to demon-
strate to the Modern Atheists of this Nation,
by this new Argument, that their sentiment
concerning the Worship of the Material and In-
sensible

senfible Heavens ; can no wife cohere with the
fenfe of Antiquity, which they fo much value,
and refpect.

For the better underftanding of what is to be
faid concerning the perfon, who Sacrifices, and
the Ceremonies us'd by him : 'Tis to be obferv'd,
that the *Northern* and *Southern* Temple, which
together make the *Tien Tan*, are two different
Buildings, whereof the Interiour is the Repofi-
tory of the Infcription containing the facred
Name, where its kept during the courfe of the
Year ; and the Exteriour, a kind of Church, or
Royal Hall of the Ceremonies, in which its expos'd on folemn occafions. Both thefe Halls are
large, folid, round buildings, Compos'd of three
Uniform Orders of Architecture, rifing in com-
ly and handfome proportion. Four Afcents lead
to thefe Halls, containing Nine Degrees, each
of nine Steps. They differ in this, that the *Nor-
thern* Hall is Crufted on the out-fide with white
Marble ; and hath plac'd under the middle of its
Roof, a round Temple, beautify'd by a triple
Yellow Roof, under which there rifes a Throne,
Dedicated to the Divine Majefty, not much different from the Emperial Throne. The *Southern*
Hall is beautify'd with Brick of an AzureColour,
and has the Heaven for Roof : But on Solemn
Days it has, in place of Roof, a Tent which is
Erected, and ferves for a Tabernacle for the facred Infcription The Ceremonies us'd before
the facred Name of the Supreme Emperour, by
the *Chinefe* Emperour himfelf. (For all Relations
agree that it belongs to him alone to offer Sacrifice in this Temple) have a great affinity with
those

those respects, which the *Mandarins* pay to this Prince in his Palace   For as they who are Keepers of this place, observ'd, as the Emperour, who during the year, is, as it were shut up in his Palace: At the beginning of the new year enters a stately Hall, and plac'd there on his Throne, has all the great Men of his Court, and the *Mandarins* of each Tribunal, all in their Ranks, and richly Clad before him, who at a sign given by all manner of Musical Instruments, bow down their heads nine times to the ground at set Intervals.   In the same manner, the sacred Inscription is brought out of the Inner Temple, its Domestick Sanctuary, into the Exterior Hall, a publick place, attended by Choirs of Musicians, and Companies of Dancers, among whom, some Emperours have not disdain'd to mix themselves

When the Sacred Name of God is plac'd upon the Throne, then the Emperour quitting his usual Garments, puts on Purple Robes, and enters the Hall, attended by the Princes, Ministers, and chief Courtiers. The remainder of his stately Retinue of *Musick* staying without, having plac'd those who enter'd with him, in decent order, he alone mounts the Steps of the Throne, not up the middle, but one the one side, (which difference is also paid him in his Palace) being come to the top of the second rank of the steps; not presuming to advance any farther, the Musick striking up, on a signal given, he Kneels down, and at set Intervals, all his numerous Retinue following his example, bows down Nine times to the ground, reverently Adoring the Divine Majesty, whom he acknowledges to be his

Emperour

Emperour and Lord He values himself so highly on this account, that he is never better pleas'd,
than when his Subjects stile him *Pi Hia*, by
which expression they signify, that tho', as they
express themselves, he is above the heads of the
World, yet he is under the steps of the Throne
of *a m T*, and Adores his Foot stool.

After this Adoration, follows a noble Sacrifice,
prepar'd in the name of the Emperour, and the
whole Empire, a publick Cryer Reading in a
loud and distinct Voice in the Emperours name,
the Form of the Oblation, and Antiphons fitted to
each Action, Sung in Musick. These Antiphons
set forth in very magnificent terms the Divine
Power, Majesty, Science, Providence, and other
Attributes and Benefits of God Our design'd
brevity doth not permit us to transcribe all; neither can we well quite omit them, we shall therefore instance some few. First then in the Solemn
Form of Offering the Sacrifice, the Emperour
uses his own proper name without any addition
of Titles, which amongst this People is the greatest Testimony which can be given of his Superiour
Dignity, who is spoken to. Then he stiles himself Servant and Subject, and says, he offers
these things to *Teu Ab ai Hinde*, the supreme
Emperour of Heaven We omit the other Contents of this Solemn Oblation, it being in the
Tartar Tongue, and consequently less known to
most Missionaries, to whom the Contents of the
Chinese Books will be more grateful. We shall
therefore Translate here some solemn Invoca-
tions us'd by the Emperour *Hia Cui*, the
Twelfth Prince of the Family *Tay Mim*, when
many years ago, he chang'd the Ancient Inscriptions

tions of these Temples, which run thus· 'To
'the supreme Lord of the Shining Heavens:
'And put in place of them this sentence, to
'the Heavenly King of Kings, and supreme
'Lord.

In 'the solemn Obligation of this Title *Ho
am*, of whom mention has been made, first
judging himself unworthy to be heard, calls upon
all Spirits, and entreats them not to disdain to
employ all their spiritual and Intellectual vertue with the Supreme Lord, in order to expose
to him the humble and submissive sentiments of his
mind, and entreat him to accept favourably this
Oblation, and Title, which he offers him pro-
strate on the Ground with all possible Respect.

On the day this Title was Dedicated to the
Supreme Emperour, the Musick Sung the following Antiphon to him, as present and approving
this Solemnity; which, tho' in the Translation
it falls short of the Energy of the *Chinese* expressions; nevertheless it expresses in magnificent
terms the Eternity of Almighty God, and his
Existence before the Hills and Hinges of the
Earth : It is worded as follows   ' In the confus'd
' Beginning of the World, there was nothing but
' a confus'd Chaos: The Five Planets, or Ele-
' ments had not yet began to run round : The
' Two Lights had not yet Shin'd : He alone stood
' in the middle; who, tho' he has neither Voice
' nor Shape, yet has Voice and Shape, as being
' the Supreme Lord of all Spirits, owing his Be-
' ing only to himself, and bringing into order this
' confus'd Mass. He in the beginning divided
' the Thick from the Thin, made Heaven, made
' Earth

' Earth, made Man, from whom afterwards pro-
' ceeded all kind of Creatures.

In the next Antiphon he says, 'Ti, i e. ' The
' Lord produc'd In, and Yam the first Principles
' of all Material things, having absolute Power
' to Create, and Produce. This Spirit produced
' the seven Planets, giving them vertue to shine
' on, and Influence Inferior things. He cover'd
' all things with the Heavens, and fixt all by the
' Immobility of the Earth, that they might en-
' joy a constant and stable state. In thanks for
' this great Benefit, I your Subject offer my hum-
' ble Adoration to you, and presume to offer to
' you Supreme Emperour, this Augustus Title
' Hoam, King of Kings.

The Oblation of the Silks and Vessels made
of precious Stones is accompany'd by this Antiphon, in which he says, 'Ti, O Lord be pleas'd
' to hear with a Fatherly Affection these desires of
' your Child, not being otherwise able to com-
' ply with this Duty of a Child towards you, the
' best of Parents. I have presum'd to present you
' this Title. And because you have been pleas'd
' to look down propitiously on this my Oblation,
' in Thanksgiving for this singular favour, I make
' bold to offer to you these few Vessels and
' Silks.

In the Fourth Antiphon, he says, 'He offers
' to the Supreme Lord, who has been pleas'd to
' regard his humble desires, the first Cup of
' Wine, in Testimony of Praise and Joy for his
' perpetual and unlimited Duration, which nei-
' ther has, nor will have its equal. In the fifth
Antiphon he complains of Men who are surround-
ed by the Benefits which they have reciev'd from
this

this Supreme Emperour· Altho', says he, 'So
'many, and so Pregnant Testimonies of this Su-
'preme Emperour's Love towards all Living
'Creatures are every where extant, yet who at-
'tentively considers the Origin from whence
'they flow? This certainly is no other than the
Supreme Emperour of all Nations, Maker of all
things, and true Creator. Omitting several others
we shall add by way of Conclusion, that which
accompanies the other of the Title, which is as
follows. 'The Supreme Lord Commanded, and
'the three Principal parts of the World were
'Made, Heaven, Earth, and Man; and all other
'things. In the middle he plac'd a Man, and all
'other Creatures I your Subject beg that the
'Deceas'd Emperours, my Fore-Fathers, whose
'Names are here, may be so happy to enjoy your
'Presence in your Heavenly Kingdom

In a word, in these and other Antiphons we
have omitted the Supreme Lord is acknowledg'd to be 'Creator, and Conservator. Eternal
'and Omnipotent, to see the secrets of Hearts,
'to reward Good, and punish Evil, and to give
'Verbum the Greatest expression, to be Holy and
'Understanding No whoever doth not
perceive in these Expressions a clear Acknowledg-
ment of God, must either be an Atheist by Inclination, or rely too much on such Mens Judgments;
and it happens but too often to some Learned
Men to meet first with Atheistical Treaties, and
not being well vers'd in other Books, to be so far
insensibly charmed with their frothy flourishes, as
to think the other not valuable, when they
are most desirable, as when they attempt to
explain the most unaccountable Effects, and
clear

clear Texts of the Ancients, which speak a loud the Existence of a God, by *Sympathy* and *Antipathy*.

Of the Temple Ti Tan.

In this Temple there is neither Image nor Idol, nor any thing like one : The Emperour himself chief Pontif, the first Ministers of the Empire, and the Keepers of this place assure us, that their Worship here is directed to the same Supreme Being, Ador'd in the *Tien Tan*. This is also evident by the Inscription expos'd the day when the Solemn Adoration is perform'd, which is this, *Ho un Tiki*, done thus in *Tartar*, *Nu Ha*, that is, Supreme Lord of the Earth. On the front are these *Chinese* Characters *Houm Ki Xe*, to whom these *Tartar* correspond *Nai Han in P to*, that is the House of the Supreme Lord of Earth. These two Inscriptions agree with those of the *Tien Tan*, already mention'd, as to the sense, and as to the words too, with their Canonical Book, call'd *Liki*, which gives the Name of *Ki* unto *Xan Ti*. These Inscriptions prove evidently, that the Ancient *Chinese* Emperours knew the true God, and that he is Ador'd by them, who rule in this present Age, and acknowledge, as the *Chinese* Characters make it evidently appear, to govern with Supreme power both Heaven and Earth. On this account the Emperour in the *Tartar* form of Offering the Sacrifice (no other being Read when he Sacrifices) says both in *Tien Tan*, and in this Temple, that he offereth all to *Hande*, or the supreme Lord ; and calls himself in express terms the Subject of this Supreme Lord. In a word, here he uses the

E   same

some reverencial expressions in Addressing himself to him, and the submissive posture of Body, and interiour demission towards the supreme Lord of Heaven and Earth.

We know very well that some Emperours of the middle Age of his Monarchy, were so impiously over-seen, as to Associate to this supreme Lord a certain Genious of the Earth, or as they call'd her *Heu Ti*., Lord of a certain Genius of the Earth, or Empress of the Earth. Amongst these was *Hoei Cum*, the Eight Prince of the Family *Sum*. But we also know that the *Chinese* Authors's sharply reprehend him in these words: By the word *Ti* in the Inscription *Xam Ti*, is meant the Lord and Governour of Heaven: None equals his excellence. Why therefore did *Hoei Cum* Associate an equal to him with a new Title? He who sins against Heaven, hath none left him, to whom he may have recourse. By which, and other following reprehensions and censures, they condemn this Emperour for the affecting a greater Impunity, than his Predecessours, by dividing the object of their Worship, and introducing a new fangled Goddess, who might protect him against the Anger of Heaven. Whereas, as they remark, the word *Ti* imports the supreme Lord and Governour of Heaven, who admits no equal.

These same proofs make it clear, that the matter, pomp and other solemnities of the Sacrifice offer'd by the Emperour at the Summer Solstice, are the same with those practis'd in the *Tien Tan*. This is certain, that in this City the same Fast, separation from their Wives, examine of their Actions, and purpose of Amendment, is Impos'd on all by

a

a Law, which exempts not the Emperour himself. There is indeed this difference betwixt the *Tien Tan*, and the *Ti Tan* : First that the Throne on which the sacred Inscription is plac'd, is round in the first, and square in the latter. Secondly, That in the *Tien Tan*, the Emperour offers that kind of Sacrifice, call'd by the *Chinese*, *Tan Chai*, and *Leao*, in which the Victims are consum'd by Fire. They esteem this kind of Sacrifice the most proper to express the power of the supreme Lord, in relation to the Production and Destruction of all things, and this Sacrifice is call'd *Kiao* But in *Ti Tan*; all the Victims are reverently Buried in the Earth ; by which Ceremony they design to express the power of the supreme Being, in conserving and cherishing all that he produc'd.

For this reason they frequently call the supreme Lord *Ta Fu Mu*, the great Father and Mother ; which is the very Name all the *Chinese* Christians give to Almighty God ; this Sacrifice they call *Xe*, so that it cannot in reason seem strange to any Man who has visited these Temples, to hear the Emperour himself, and the chief Men of the Empire affirm, that not only the Ancients, but they themselves Adore the supreme Lord of Heaven, and not the Material Inanimate Globes; that both of their usual and customary Sacrifices are directed to him, and that to express this their intent, they make use of *Confucius* his words, without naming him, taken out of his Canonical Book *Chum Yum*, where he says, ' That *Kiao Xe* is the Worship paid to the su- ' preme Lord.

On

On this occasion we muſt take notice with many *Chineſe* Doctors of the extreme boldneſs of that Atheiſtical head of the *Chineſe* Politicians *Hoe. Chu*, who falſify'd this clear Text, which incommoded him by adding *Heu Tu* to it: whence ſober and thinking Men may gather how far theſe Commentaries are to be rely'd on ; and whether all they advance is to be look'd on as certain 'Tis very certain that in the decernment of Commentaries, thoſe are to be rejected, which are contrary to the plain ſenſe of the Text ; and by ſtrain'd Gloſſes endeavour to give it a different meaning, from what the words import, and at the ſame time interfer with themſelves, and that not obſcurely and rarely, but very frequently, and in a manner obvious to the meaneſt capacities. Now the moſt Learned Men of the Empire, and the Doctors of the Royal Academy charge theſe new Gloſſes with theſe Capital Faults : And hence 'tis become a Proverb amongſt the Learned ; *Believe the Text, but don't believe the Gloſs.* What has been ſaid concerning the Emperours Offering Sacrifice in the *Tien Tar*, muſt be alſo underſtood of this Temple ; for as he only offers the Sacrifice *Kiao* in the *Tien Tu* ; ſo he alone offers the Sacrifice *Xe* in the *Ti Tan*, in the Name of the whole Empire, and as they ſay, of the whole World From him alone the Feudatary Kings reciev'd formerly, together with the Royal Enſigns, as Governours of Towns do at this day, the Authority to offer *Xe*, but with this difference, that the Solemnities allow d them are limited, in proportion to their reſpective Dignities : in ſo much, that they only offer ſacrifice for thoſe under their Juriſdiction, and

dare

dare not fo much as call upon the Tutelar Spirits of other places : Whence the Imperial Sacrifice is call'd in their Canonical Book, *Liki Ta Xe,* or the Great and Univerfal Sacrifice.

And thus much concerning thefe Sacrifices, which, tho' unlawful upon many accounts, efpeally fince the Inftitution of that which the Church of Chrift doth ufe, yet have been juftly infifted upon, becaufe they conduce to the clearing the matter in hand, and furnifh a ftrong Argument againft the *Chinefe* Atheifts. 'Tis fufficient for us to have demonftrated by the Teftimonies of the Minifters of thefe Sacrifices, by the Infcriptions of thefe Temples, and their Tranflation done and approv d by publick Authority, by the previous pieparations, the folemn Forms of their Oblation, and other Rites obferv'd in them ; that the Ancient and prefent *Chinefe* Monaichs Sacifice not to the Material Heavens, and Earth, as their Canonical Book *Liki* affiims in thefe exprefs teims : Heaven hath not two Suns, nor one Country two Kings, neither are thefe Sacrifices Inftituted to honour two Lords.

We make no mention here of the other Temples, *Ge Tan,* and *Gue Tan,* Built heretofore within this City · Becaufe they are not Dedicated to the Supieme Loid ; but to the greater and leffer Luminous Angelical Spirits, and different and inferiour Rites are us'd in them, as the *Mandeiins,* who aie Keepers of them, affuie us.

Otier

*Other Testimonies of the knowledge of God, drawn
from popular Tradition.*

It will not be unfeasonable to add to this Royal and Publick Tradition, some further proofs of this Truth, drawn from the manner and object of the Worship obferv'd by the People for the knowledge of the true God; for this was not fo confin'd to the Royal Family, as to be quite conceal'd from the Vulgar, as will appear by two Inftances: The firft of which fhall be taken from what is practis'd in many private Families, and the fecond from certain forms of fpeech us'd amongft the People.

In many Commoners Houfes, and in thofe too of fome Learned Men, this Infcription confifting of Ten *Chinefe* Characters, is expos'd to the Families Veneration, *Tien, Ti, San Kiai, Xefam, Van Lim ChinCay,* that is, the true Lord of Heaven and Earth, the Three Regions, Ten Divifions, and all Intellectual Beings Now whether by the Three Regions of the Air, they mean the Supreme, Middle, and Inferiour Regions, and by the Ten Divifions, the Ten parts, the Ancient *Chinefe* Syftem, reprefented by the figure *Ho Tu,* divided the World into, or fome other Divifion: 'Tis ftill certain, that this Infcription fpeaks of the true Lord, and Governour of all things, and that in fuch clear and expreffive terms, as cannot be baffled by any Cavils or Gloffes Three forts of People pay refpect to this Infcription · Some have neither Statue nor Idol in their Houfes, are addicted to no Sect, Adore none of the Pagan Gods , in a word, admit of no other Worfhip,

then

than what they pay before this Title of Supreme
Lord, which they take care to place very decent-
ly, by burning Perfumes, and Prostrations, and
if we may measure the customs of other Provinces, by this Town and Province: We may. conclude there are innumerable People of all Sects
and Professions, who not only have this Inscription in their Houses, which is not appropriated to
any Sect in particular; but also honour it by
burning Perfumes and other Ceremonies, tho' at
times, and they all agree in preferring it before any
Idol, and honour it in a different place out of
their Houses, and judging them unworthy to
contain the Name of the Supreme Lord of Majesty,
therefore they fix it on, or over their Doors, that
they may be always put in mind by the sight of it,
to Worship this Supreme Lord above all things.
There are others, tho' but few, who joyn to Fi-
gures of their Idols, this Inscription, and by this
means apply to Fictitious Beings, the sense of
what belongs to the true God alone   Tables containing this Inscription, but differently Adorn'd
are expos'd to Sale, at the end of each Year thro'
the whole Empire, to the end, every one may be
provided with them , and all unanimously joyn
in the Worship of it on the first day of the new
Year   At which time over and above the Burning
of Perfumes, and other usual Ceremonies ;
Raw Rice, Fruits, and other Comestibles are
offer'd before this Inscription to the Supreme
Lord of all things, either in Thanksgiving for the
Nourishment they have receiv'd from him, or in
order to obtain it for the future, and then own
Canonical ritual Orders the Emperour to beg of
the supreme Lord a Plentiful Harvest.   We omit

its

its many clear Texts, relating to this Infcription ;
it not being our prefent defign to write the Hi-
ftory of its Origen and Propagation   This one
thing relating to the point in Queftion, is certain,
viz. That this Writing contains a clear notion of
the True God; and what is very remarkable, the
Chinefe Annals, and other publick Monuments,
which give an exact account of the Rife and Pro-
grefs of all the different Sects which have been
in this Empire, give no account when the ufe of
this Infcription began, which feems an evident
Proof of the knowledge of the true God, having been time out of mind amongft this People,
where yet it remains pure from all mixture or I-
dolatry in many Families

The other Head, which may juftly be reckon'd
amongft the Proofs extant in this Empire, of its
enjoying the knowledge of the True God, contains certain forms of Speech in ufe amongft thefe
People   Thefe are of two different forts, fome
being proper to the Learnd, others common a-
mongft the People: We fhall at prefent compare
them together, in order to make it clear, that
they agree as to the fenfe, tho' they differ in
words.   For the People prcceeding with down
right Simplicity, exprefs by many, and obvious
words, what the Learned affect to fay in a Laco-
rick and Figurative way.   Now it is not to be
imagin'd, that when the Learned in lieu of naming God, the Emperour the Prefident, and
Members of a Tribunal, and the like, ufe the
Names of the places they refide in   It is not, I
fay, to be imagin'd, that in thefe occafions the
People do not underftand their true meaning ;
or think, when they hear them fay, that the juft

Court

Court is to be honour'd, that they speak of the place where the Affembly is held, and not of thofe who are Members and Heads of it; they know very well the contrary, and efpecially when the Emperour is fpoak of, by the Name of the Chief Hall of the Palace, and Almighty God is mention'd by the Name of Heaven; for thefe fignres are grown fo Familiar to them by ufe, that they leave no more doubt of his meaning, who ufes them, than if he employ'd the common and ufual expreffions, which are more frequent amongft the commonalty.

This Phrafe is common among the People, *Lao Tien Ye,* that is Ancient, or Heavenly Father, or Lord of Heaven: For where we fay *Lord,* the *Chinefe* fay *Le,* and *Lao Ye;* and the People of *Pekin,* (whofe Dialect we fhall ufe in the Vulgar Expreffions, we fhall mention by *Lao,*) commonly underftand Father. Now that in thefe expreffions, *Tien* fignifies Heavenly, or of Heaven, and is not to be taken for the word Heaven in the Nominative Cafe, is evidently made out, by the *Tartar* Tranflations of the *Chinefe* Infcriptions, confifting of the indeclinable *Chinefe* words, which were perform'd by Men eminent for their fkill in both the Languages, and where the words are, *The fupreme Lord of Heaven,* and not *Heaven the fupreme Lord.* But the genuine fenfe of thefe expreffions is not fo much to be meafur'd by the rigour of Grammatical conftruction, as by what they attribute to the Ancient Father And here *Europeans* altogether ignorant of the *Chinefe* Tongue, may be competent Judges, to whom we leave it to determine; whether the great ex_ellencies attributed by them to

Hea-

Heaven; do not rather agree with God himself, than with the senseless Orbs.

The Learned commonly use this word *Tien*, *Heaven*, to which they joyn the following Epithets, *Xin Tien*, the Spiritual and Intellectual Heaven; *Cim Tien*, the piercing, or penetrating Heaven; *Cao ve chu*, the Creator, and Lord; *Ouu Cu*, Lord and Governour, &c The meaning of which will appear, by the Qualities they Attribute to Heaven.

In order to let, the Reader perceive at one cast of an Eye, that these Expressions have come down to this Age from the first foundation of this Monarchy; we shall add to every expression of the People, and the Learned some short Text taken out of their Canonical Books, omitting those which are longer, as no ways necessary here, as not being clearer than the Emperour's Declaration, which affirms in express terms, that not the Material Heaven, but the Lord, and Creator of Heaven and Earth is Ador'd. For no terms can more Emphatically express the true God; since the Prince himself, and the People knew very well, that by these words of our Exposition of the *Chinese* Rites offer'd to him, we mean the true God In the adjoyning Texts, and others omitted, these expressions are very frequent, *Ti*, Lord, supreme Lord. *Hoam*, supreme Lord, or King of Kings. *Hoi Tien*, the greatest Heaver *Xan Tien*, the supreme Heaven *Min Tien*, the merciful *Cao Cao*, the most High. *Tam Tan*, immense. *Hao Hao*, the Greatest. *Mim Mim*, the most Understanding *Yeu Yeu*, Eternal. *Cam Cam*, the most Ancient *Hoam Hoam*, the most Supreme. *He Ho*, of August Majesty, &c

W

We shall add here a List of some common expressions, omitting many more to avoid being tedious Which affirm;

First, That God lives above.

Over our heads is one Ancient Heavenly Father *People.*

Over our heads is a perspicatious Heaven. *Learned.*

The most high Lives above *Liber canonicus Xi Xim.*

Secondly, All things are produc'd by Heaven.

What is there, that was not produc'd by the Ancient Heavenly Father, and given Man for his Sustinance. *People.*

Heaven produc'd all things to nourish Man. *Learned.*

All things have their Origin from Heaven *Lib. can. Li Ki.*

Thirdly, That Heaven produc'd Man.

Who of Mankind is not produc'd by the Ancient Heavenly Father. *People.*

All Men are produc'd by Heaven *Learned.*

Heaven produc'd all Nations. *Lib. can. Xi Kim.*

Fourthly, That the Emperour has his Authority from Heaven.

Thanks be to the Heavenly Father, who has given us the best of Emperour's, and most tender of his People *People.*

The

Learned. The Sun of Heaven the Emperour, by power given from Heaven, governs peaceably the Empire.

Lib. can.
Xu Kim. Heaven has fent me down to Govern and Teach the People, and in a manner, to help the fupreme Lord to blefs the Four Quarters of the World.

Fifthly, That Heaven is to be Worship'd.

People. Who dares refufe to Worship the Heavenly Father.

Learned. Who dares fay I Adore not Heaven.

Lib. can.
Xu Kim. The fupreme Lord is to be Worship'd and ferv'd.

Sixthly, That Heaven commands mutual fervices and refpects.

People. Who contemns Man, contemns the Heavenly Father.

Learned. Who contemns Man, contemns Heaven.

Lib. can.
Su Xu. If I contemn any one, I contemn Heaven.

Seventhly, That Heaven is every where.

People. Where is not the Heavenly Father.

Learned. Over our Doors, and within our Chambers, there is a perfpicatious Heaven.

Lib. can.
Xi Kim. The greateft Heaven is call'd Intelligent, wherever you go, it prefently attains you. The greateft Heaven is
call'd

call'd Illuftrating, wherever your
thoughts carry you; thither it immediately reaches

Eighthly, That Heaven is Ignorant
of nothing.

The Heavenly Father knows what- *People.*
ever is done in private

A thought rifes in your heart, Hea- *Learned.*
ven knows it

Heaven alone is endow'd with a per- *Lib. can.*
fect Underftanding. *Xu Kim.*

Ninthly, That Heaven knows the
heart of man.

No Man knows the heart of Man, *People.*
whether it be juft, or wicked: Only
the Heavenly Father knows that.

Only the Heaven above knows the *Learned.*
heart of Man, whether it be juft or
wicked.

The fupreme Lord knows in his *Lib. can.*
heart, who are to be belov d, who are *Xu Kim.*
to be rejected, or who are good, who
are evil.

Tenthly, That Heaven rewards and
punifhes.

The Heavenly Father punifhes this *People.*
Man, and rewards the other.

Heaven undoubtedly rewards the *Learned.*
Juft, and punifhes the Wicked.

'Tis the Law of Heaven to profper *Lib. can.*
good Men, and to afflict the Wicked. *Xu Kim.*

11thly,

11thly, That Heaven fees perfectly all things

People. The Heavenly Father fees things truly, as they are in themfelves.

Learned. The Heaven above fees things truly.

Lib. can.
Xi Kim. The fupreme Lord vieweth with great Clarity the Four Regions of the World.

12thly, That Heaven hath an Eye upon Men.

People. The Ancient Heavenly Father looks down hither

Learned. There is a Heaven above which looks on us

Lib can.
Xi Kim. Only Heaven views the People fubject to it.

13. That Heaven hears.

People. There is an Ancient Heavenly Father, who hears.

Learned. The word which is Whifper'd in fecret, founds as loud as Thunder in the Ears of Heaven.

Lib. can.
Kiao-yiu The found of good works reaches to Heaven; rejoyceth the heart of the Heavenly Father.

14. That Heaven cannot be deciev'd.

People. Man may be deciev'd, but the Heavenly Father cannot.

Man

Man may be deciev'd, but not Hea- *Learned.*
ven.

Comprehending by perfect under- *Lib. can.*
standing what's below, and illustrating *Xⁱ Kim.*
with August Glory what's above.

15. That Heaven hates the Wicked.

The Heavenly Father suffers not cor- *People.*
rupted Men.

Heaven above is Angry with the *Learned.*
Wicked

Who Sins against Heaven, hath none *Lib. can.*
left him, to whom he may have re- *Su Xio.*
course

16. That Heaven hates the Proud.

The Heavenly Father hath confound- *People.*
ed my proud Thoughts, and humbled
me.

Heaven suffereth not the Proud. *Learned.*

Heaven hates the Proud, and loves *Lib. can.*
the Humble. *Y Kim.*

17 That Heaven is Juſt.

The Heavenly Father is Juſt. *People.*

Heaven is moſt Juſt, and free from all *Learned.*
exceptions of perſons

The Supreme Lord is free from all *Lib. c.and*
exceptions of perſons, and only values *Xu Kim.*
Vertue.

18. That Heaven is to be obey-
ed.

In ·

People.   In obedience to the Heavenly Father's will *Item.* I give my life to the Heavenly Father.

Learned.   Nothing happens which Heaven hath not decreed. A wise Man obeys Heaven.

Lib. can.   We must acquiess to the pleasure and
Xu Kim. command of Heaven.

19. That Heaven comforteth the Good.

People.   The Heavenly Father permits not the hopes of the Just to be frustrated.

Learned.   The supreme Lord of Heaven doth not decieve the hopes of the Just

Lib. can.   The supreme Lord of Heaven aslists
Xu Kim. the Good.

20. That Heaven has mercy on us.

People.   Ancient Father of Heaven, have mercy on us, and that sufficeth.

Learned.   Heaven will, I hope, have mercy on us.

Lib. can.   Merciful Heaven is to be call'd upon
Su Xu. with Sighs.

21. That Pardon is to be hop'd for from Heaven.

People.   I beg the Heavenly Father to pardon me, and that is all I desire.

Learned.   Heaven gives Men time to grow Wise, and Repent.

Lib. can.   Contrition is the Key of Hea-
Xu Kim. ven.   22. That

2   That Heaven is to be fear'd.

Fear you not the Heavenly Fa- *People.*
ther ?

Heaven which is above is to be fea- *Learn'd.*
red.

The Majesty of Heaven is to be fea- *Lib. can.*
red or dreaded.   *Xu Kim.*

23 That the Counsels of Heaven are
above our reach.

No man can know the Counsels of *People.*
the Heavenly Father.

The resolves of Heaven are very pro- *Learned.*
found, and hard to be understood.

The resolves of the Supreme Heaven *Lib. can.*
have neither Sound nor smell, by which *Xi Kim.*
they may be perceiv'd.

24. That Heaven hath its ways of
reckoning.

The different ways of mens reckon- *People.*
ing, can prevail nothing against the
reckoning of the Heavenly Father.

Heaven hath its Rules of Addition, *Learned.*
Substraction, Multiplication, and Divi-
sion.

The Supreme Lord is without con- *Lib. can.*
trole : his Commands are never given *Kia Yu.*
in Vain.

25 That events depend on Heaven.

That our endeavours prove Succesful, *People.*
is entirely owing to the Heavenly Father.

F   It

Learned.   It belongs to men to undertake ; but it belongs to Heaven to give success to their Undertakings.

Lib car.
Su Xi.   Heaven is cause of those things, whose cause we are ignorant of.

26 That Heaven is absolute Lord of Life and Death.

People.   Upon a man's designing me mischief, I do not Immediately die : but if the Heavenly Father will have me die ; die I must.

Learned.   Heaven being willing I should live, no man can hurt me: But if Heaven condemns me, who can deliver me?

Lib. car.
Su An.   If Heaven Condemns me not to die, what harm can my adversary of the Kingdom *Quam* do me.

27. That Heaven dispenses Riches and Poverty.

People   If it please the Heavenly Father I shall prosper ; if not, I shall not.

Learned.   That some are happy, others miserable, proceeds entirely from Heaven.

Lib car.
Su Xu.   Riches and Honours depend on Heaven

28. That Heaven is to be call'd upon as witness.

People.   The Heavenly Father sees my heart, and that is enough.

I

I need not blush, since Heaven sees *Learned.* my heart.

Let Heaven hate me; may Heaven *Lib. can.* hate me, if it be not so.   *Su Xu.*

The Reader hath in this small Treatise, Three things of moment, in relation to the Matter of Fact in Question; that is, to the sense and meaning of the *Chinese* in their Worship of Heaven, *Confucius*, and their Ancestors.

In the first place, the Emperours Declaration couch'd in such terms, and given in such circumstances, as render it clear and safe beyond exception. And its being Printed in the publick News Books, Register'd among the Royal Acts, and presented to the chief Ministers and Presidents of the Tribunals of the Empire, gives an unquestionable Authority and certainty. The Reader may understand by this Declaration, how undeservedly this Prince, to whom Religion ows so much, hath been defam'd in *Europe*, as an Athiest. And truly, could not this Injurious Aspersion, which has been strengthen'd by so many Conjectures, and study'd Reasons, be effectually prov'd false, it would be certainly very prejudicial to the common belief of a God in these parts, upon account of the repute this Prince is in for his Learning, and the weight of his Authority in Decisions of this nature. This is so very great, that either thro' respect or flattery, both the *Tartars* and *Chinese* look upon all Royal Edicts, which they call *Chi Y*, as Oracles.

On this account we durft not endeavour to add Authority to his Decifion, by adjoyning their Approbations.

In the second place we have produc'd many and clear Teftimonies, in order to illuftrate and confirm this Royal fentence to thofe of *Europe*, who are not acquainted with the force it hath here. Now thefe Teftimonies are not Texts of their own Canonical Books; many of which proving clearly our Opinion, have been cited in Printed Apologies ; nor given by *Chinefe* Chriftians, who adhere to our Opinion, who in Number, Dignity, and Learning, far furpafs thofe who are againft it, but by Infidels now living, who have pafs'd thro' all their different degrees, and have obtain'd the Supreme Dignities of the Empire, and being in thefe eminent Pofts, may be confulted by feveral ways. Whence it is manifeft, that it is a notorious falfity, and a mere begging of the Queftion, to pretend that thofe gloffes of the Impious *Chinefe*, who fay that the Ancients fpoak of the Material Heavens, cannot be rejected ; fince the moft Learned Men of the Empire, not only reject them, but declare them no ways confonant to the fenfe of the Ancients. This we can affirm upon our certain knowledge, that we never yet confulted any Doctors of this Nation (and we have confulted many, tho' of an inferiour rank) concerning the Worfhip of Heaven, whofe Sentiments did not perfectly agree with the Teftimonies of thofe eminent Men we have cited, in exploding as erroneous their opinion, who pretend, that the Material Heaven

is

is meant, when mention is made of the Worſhip that is to be pay'd to Heaven.

In the Third place we have given ſtrong
proofs of the knowledge of the true God, drawn
from the Tradition of the royal Family, and
the commonalty; which yet remains in ſpite of
the many Superſtitions, which have crept in;
now theſe put together, will evidently make out
that this Noble and Ancient Empire grounded
on ſuch excellent Laws, as are ſtill in force in
it, owes not its Foundation to Athieſts.   And
hence our *Europian* Athieſt, will be no longer
able to uſe it as an inſtance againſt Divines;
who prove that Atheiſm is a neceſſary cauſe of
publick Trouble and Miſeries; and ruins all
manner of Government. Finally, it will evidently
appear by theſe Teſtimonies, that Divine Providence preſerv'd the firſt Fathers and Founders
of the *Chineſe* Church for many years from er-
ring, even as to the matter of fact in queſtion,
and gave them ſo perfect an underſtanding of
the Claſſick books of this Nation; that their
many and Learned Treatiſes on all manner of
Subjects, are the only, which appear in the Royal Library; the only which are Studied by
the Princes, and Chief Doctors of the Empire;
and what favors of a Prodigy (conſidering the
innate Pride of this People, and their hate of Externs) in the Tribunal of the Mathematicks, there
are Sixty Volumes of their Compoſition, relating
to that Science, which are the only made and ſtu-
died by the *Chineſe* and *Tarter* Doctors, ſo that on
the one hand they are highly valued by the Learned Chriſtians : and they have on the other for
their ſentiment the Chief Doctors of the Empire.
                                                                Now

Now if they, who flight fo much thefe able men, were in any repute amongst the Learned of this Empire upon account of their skill in the Language and Antiquities of this Nation, they might indeed upon their Teftimony and Efteem, be admitted to contend with the firft founders of this Miffion, concerning matters, whofe decifion depends entirely on this fort of Learning, but will never be thought fit to enter thefe lifts with them, on the account of the praifes given them by their friends in *Europe*. In the mean time it is evident by what has been faid, that the Infcription *Kien Tien* is not to be underftood of the Material Heavens; and the ufual Honours paid to *Confucius* and the Dead, are only Civil Ceremonies, and Teftimonies of Gratitude. Now the only reafon which has prevail'd on men eminent for Vertue and Learning, to labour in the defence of this truth, is, that the contrary opinion will hinder many, and efpecially the learned from embracing Chriftianity; and expofe this Miffion to evident danger of being depriv'd of all their affiftance, who labour in it

But whereas we underftand that fome not only flight this danger, but endeavour alfo to leffen it in others apprehenfions, by what they write into *Europe* We, who of different Nations are here together, and Labour in the Gofpel; and have before our eyes the Laws of this Court, and are acquainted with their Sentiments, who govern the Empire, do difcharge our confciences by this publick Proteftation; by which we declare, that the Church of *China* cannot long fubfift, in cafe the Rites, by which this people Honour *Confucius*, and the Dead, be no longer permitted in the Sense we have explain'd them. We moreover Judge, as things stand at present, that the first accusation made by any Malicious person, concerning the present differences about them, will certainly hasten the ruine of this Mission We thought it necessary to conclude this Treatise with this protestation, least it might be objected to the Society, that we gave not timely notice of this great and threatning danger: which we do at present, by subscribing this Protestation at *Pekin* the 29th. of *July* in the Year 1701.

Anthony Thomas, Vice Provincial of *China.*
Phillippe Grimaldi, Rector of the College at *Pekin.*
Thomas Pereyra.
John Francis Gerbillon.
Joseph Suares.
Joachim Bouvet.
Kiliamus Stumpf.
Baptista Regy.
Lewis Pernetti.
Dominick Paremn.
All Priests of the Society of J E S U S.

F I N I S

Lightning Source UK Ltd.
Milton Keynes UK
UKOW07f1905041017
310424UK00005B/449/P